CHRISTOPHER
COLUMBUS
THE VOYAGE OF DISCOVERY 1492

SAMUEL ELIOT MORISON

CHRISTOPHER COLUMBUS

THE VOYAGE OF DISCOVERY 1492

DORSET PRESS

Text by Samuel Eliot Morison excerpted from *The European Discovery of America: The Southern Voyages, 1492-1616*, Copyright © 1974 by Samuel Eliot Morison.

This edition published by
Dorset Press,
a division of Marboro Books Corp.,
by arrangement with Brompton Books Corporation.

Produced by Brompton Books Corporation
15 Sherwood Place
Greenwich, CT 06830

Copyright © 1991 Brompton Books Corporation

ISBN 0-88029-589-9

Printed in Hong Kong

PAGE ONE: Plaster relief of Columbus made for the World Columbia Exhibition in Chicago in 1893.

PAGE TWO: A cartographer at work, as shown in a fifteenth-century print.

THESE PAGES: a woodcut from the Latin edition of Columbus's 1493 Letter to Sanchez reporting on the First Voyage.

CONTENTS

INTRODUCTION

Samuel Eliot Morison (1887-1976) is universally acknowledged to have been the greatest American naval historian of the twentieth century, and probably of any century. He was the author of 26 distinguished works (one of them 15 volumes in length) and was co-author of three others. In addition to twice winning the Pulitzer Prize he received many other honors, among them the Presidential Medal of Freedom and the Bancroft Prize. For some 40 years he was one of the most prominent members of the faculty of Harvard University, and before his death he attained the rank of admiral in the United States Navy. An avid yachtsman, Morison made a point of trying to sail many of the seas about which he wrote in his maritime histories, and this practical experience contributed much to the literary style for which he became famous. As one *New York Times* book reviewer wrote (of *The European Discovery of America: The Northern Voyages*): "To read this book is to be a privileged passenger on the bridge beside a master mariner who . . . imparts the wisdom of the deep in tones of salty tang – brisk, skeptical, yet always measured."

A Bostonian, Morison was educated at Harvard University, where he received his AB degree in 1908 and his PhD in 1912. He began teaching at Harvard in 1915, then joined the U.S. Army as a private in World War I, and subsequently served in the American delegation at the Paris Peace Conference. The first of his major historical works, *The Maritime History of Massachusetts, 1783-1860*, was published in 1921. The next year he was appointed Harmsworth professor of American history at Oxford University, where he remained until 1925. He then returned to the faculty of Harvard, now as a full professor, and would remain there for the remainder of his academic career.

He had already shown that he was a first-class historian; now he proved that he was an astonishingly prolific one as well. His two-volume *Oxford History of the United States* appeared in 1927, and in 1930, *Builders of the Bay Colony*, as well as the two-volume *Growth of the American Republic*, co-authored with Henry Steele Commager and William Leuchtenburg. In the 1930s he produced a four-volume *Tercentennial History of Harvard University*, followed by a one-volume condensation of the same material (*Three Centuries of Har-*

OPPOSITE: In retracing Columbus's route Morison visited hundreds of out-of-the-way places like this Venezuelan lagoon.

BELOW: Samuel Eliot Morison in his US Navy uniform.

vard, 1936), and in 1940 he published the first of his famous histories of the great voyages of discovery: *Portuguese Voyages to America Before 1500*. Two years later he brought forth the book that won him his first Pulitzer Prize, *Admiral of the Ocean Sea: A Life of Christopher Columbus.*

What set *Admiral of the Ocean Sea* decisively apart from any previous account of Columbus's voyages was the almost uncanny way in which it created in readers' imaginations the sense of "being there." In part, of course, this was due to Morison's skill as a writer, but in part it was also due to the fact that he himself *had* been there. In preparation for the book he had retraced – always under sail – every mile of Columbus's itinerary, crossing the Atlantic in the barquentine *Capitana* and then cruising up and down the Caribbean in his ketch *Otis*. Although it is not difficult to infer from his writing how this experience affected Morison, he was also characteristically explicit about it: "There is nothing like a personal visit to newly discovered lands to bring home to one the pioneers' dangers and difficulties. My admiration for them increases with time. For years I have been living with the records of heroic navigators and with the ordinary grousing, grumbling, believing but blaspheming mariner. God bless 'em all! The world will never see their like again."

By the time *Admiral of the Ocean Sea* was published America had been swept into the inferno of World War II. Somehow the 55-year-old Morison was able to secure a lieutenant commander's commission in the Navy and was promptly named the official historian of US naval operations. This appointment would ultimately (1962) result in the massive 15-volume *History of US Naval Operations in World War II*, probably the best, and certainly the most readable, official history ever written.

In addition to his continuing work on *US Naval Operations*, the prodigious Morison managed to publish no less than six other books during the decade of the 1950s. The last of these, *John Paul Jones: A Sailor's Biography* (1959), won him his second Pulitzer Prize.

He was able to maintain this amazing productivity to the end of his days. Between 1960 and his death in 1976 new Morison titles appeared at the rate of nearly one

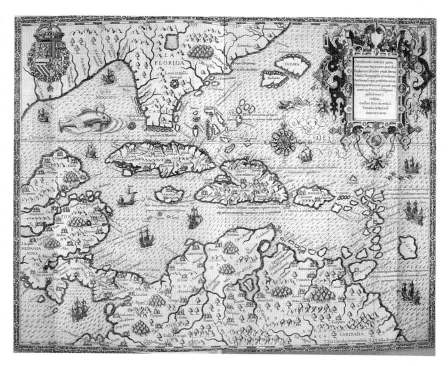

per year, and his last book, again co-authored with Henry Steel Commager, was published the year after his death.

Of these later books two, especially, are regarded as classics: *The European Discovery of America: The Northern Voyages* (1971) and *The European Discovery of America: The Southern Voyages* (1974). Once again Morison insisted on retracing routes and seeing coastlines and landfalls for himself. Before his researches were finished he had sailed the waters that interested him in ships of the US Navy and the US Coast Guard, as well as in those of the navies of Great Britain, Brazil, Argentina and Chile. In addition, in a chartered plane he had flown down the Atlantic shores of Latin America as far as Paraguay, making a comprehensive photographic record of the coast and offshore islands. From these first-hand investigations he discovered a wealth of new facts about the actual routes taken by the great explorers.

The text of the present book is excerpted from *The European Discovery of America: The Southern Voyages*, a book which, *The New York Times* wrote, "climaxes a historian's career which itself merits a place in history." It represents Morison's final word, updated and reconsidered, on the subject that had fascinated him all his life and that had first made him famous 32 years earlier: Christopher Columbus.

The Editor

ABOVE: De Bry's 1594 map of the region that Columbus had discovered a century earlier.

OPPOSITE: The massive Columbus monument that now stands at palos de la Frontera. It was from here that Columbus set out on his epic First Voyage.

CHRISTOPHER COLUMBUS

The African Background

PAGES 10-11: Genoa's Columbus Movement.

ABOVE: Europe, Asia and North Africa appear as one continent in this 1483 map based on the theories of the fifth-century philosopher Macrobius.

TOP RIGHT: A twelfth-century Arabic world map. North is at the bottom.

BELOW: Some fifteenth-century instruments for mariners, as sketched by Leonardo da Vinci.

On 12 October 1492, when the little fleet of Christopher Columbus raised a Bahamian island that he named San Salvador, neither he nor anyone else guessed that this would be an historic date. Even Columbus, who regarded himself as a child of destiny, thought he had merely found an outlying island to "the Indies." Had his entire fleet been wrecked, nobody would have been the wiser, and in all probability America would not have been discovered until 1500 when Pedro Alvares Cabral, on his way to the real India, sighted a mountain near the coast of Brazil. Thus, the entire history of Europeans in America stems from Columbus's First Voyage. The Northmen's discovery of Newfoundland almost five centuries earlier proved to be dead-end. Pre-Columbian Portuguese, Welsh, Irish, English, and Venetian voyages to America are modern-made myths, phantoms which left not one footprint on the sands of time. But Columbus's First Voyage proved to be the avant-garde for thousands of hidalgos who, weary of sustaining their haughty pride in poverty, were ready to hurl themselves on the New World in search of gold and glory.

Columbus's discovery led within a year to the first permanent European colony in America, in Hispaniola; and he himself made three more voyages of discovery, as well as sparking off those of Ojeda, Juan de La Cosa, the younger Pinzón, Vespucci, both Cabots, Magellan, and countless others. Not only the northern voyages, starting with John Cabot's of 1497, but the southern voyages of discovery and Spain's vast empire stretching from Florida to Patagonia and out to the Philippines stem from the First Voyage of that intrepid mariner and practical dreamer Christopher Columbus, Admiral of the Ocean Sea.*

Just as these southern voyages flow from Columbus's First, of 1492, so that was an indirect result of Portuguese voyages south along the west coast of Africa and out to the Madeiras and Azores. This had been going on since about 1430, when the Infante Dom Henrique (Prince Henry the Navigator) established himself at Sagres near Cape St. Vincent "where endeth land and where beginneth sea," as the great Portuguese poet Camoëns described it. There, a natural place for ships on all north-south routes to anchor, he set up a sort of information service where shipmasters might consult the latest charts and pick up useful data about wind and currents. This was no "naval academy" or "astronomical observatory" as some of the Infante's more enthusiastic biographers have maintained, but he did encourage the bolder navigators and reward new discoveries out of his royal revenues, with such success that his nephew D. Afonso V and great-nephew D. João II, kings of Portugal, carried on the good work after his death in 1460.

It took some time before D. Henrique could persuade anyone to round Cabo de

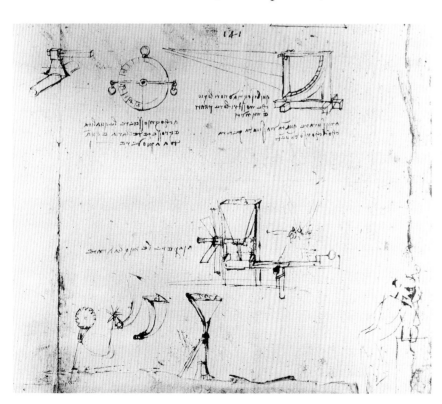

*Since ancient times Ocean had been regarded as one and indivisible.

PRINCE HENRY
OF
PORTUGALL

CEUTA

Portugal's Henry the Navigator, as imagined by an English artist some 300 years later. The evidence suggests that Henry was in fact beardless and rather thin of face. But that he was history's first great royal patron of exploration is at least a matter not open to debate.

Não* on the western bulge of Africa, because of two superstitions: that one would never get back again against the prevailing northerlies, and that anyone who persisted would run into boiling hot water

*In English called Cape Nun, and subject of the punning verse:

Quem passar o Cabo Não
Ou voltará ou não
When old Cape Nun heaves into sight
Turn back, me lad, or else – good night!

It was, apparently, the next cape after the better known Bojador.

at the Equator. Finally Gil Eanes, a Portuguese captain, rounded this cape in 1434 and found that the reputed terrors of the southern ocean did not exist, and that with a new type of ship, the caravel, one could beat to windward and get back. Within a few years ships had gone far enough along West Africa to trade for black slaves and gold dust, and the Portuguese had erected a fortified trading factory on Arguin Island near latitude 20° N. By 1460, when the Infante died, his caravels had passed the site

A fifteenth-century engraving of a carrack, a ship type to which Columbus's *Santa Maria* probably belonged.

of Dakar and were within hailing distance of Sierra Leone, only ten degrees above the Equator.

It is still a matter of controversy whether or not D. Henrique consciously sought India by circumnavigating Africa. The Pope did indeed grant Portugal in 1455 exclusive jurisdiction over the coast of Guinea "and past that southern shore all the way to the Indians": but did he mean the real India or only the "Hither India" of Prester John? That mythical Christian potentate was supposed to hold sway somewhere in western Asia or northern Africa. The substance behind this legend was Ethiopia; but in European imagination Prester John was a more wealthy and powerful monarch than any of their own princes. Contact with him was ardently desired in order to kindle a Christian backfire against the infidel Turk. Columbus once thought he was hot on the trail of Prester John in Cuba!

For almost a decade after Prince Henry's death the Portuguese made no great progress southward, except to settle the Cape Verde Islands. Then, in 1469, D. Afonso V gave a Lisbon merchant named Fernão

Gomes the monopoly of trading with the Guinea coast, on condition that he explore a hundred leagues farther every year. And there is no doubt that by this time the crown was seeking a southern sea route to India. Gomes's vessels promptly swung around the bulge and opened up the richest part of West Africa: the Gold and Ivory Coasts and Malagueta, where a variety of pepper almost as hot as the East Indian was found. By 1474, when his monopoly expired, Fernão Gomes had sent ships clean across the Gulf of Guinea and reached the island of Fernando Po on latitude 3° 30' N, where the African coast again turns southward.

In this African exploration the Portuguese developed a type of small sailing ship that they named *caravella*, the caravel. We know little of its hull design or construction, which, combined with its lateen sail plan, enabled the caravel to sail closer to the wind and faster than any square-rigger. This capability enabled a mariner to go as far as he pleased along the African coast, with assurance that he could get back. A long reach on the starboard tack, which the Portuguese called *a volta do mar largo*,

A fifteenth-century print showing ship-building in a port in north Europe. Naval architecture here was not as developed as in the south, a fact that favored the Portuguese and Spanish in the race for discovery.

would take her from the Canaries or the west coast of Africa to the Azores, where she could replenish at the port of Angra in Terceira and catch a good slant for Lisbon.

This long hitch off soundings taught the Portuguese mariners confidence and led to the development of celestial navigation – shooting the sun or the North Star with astrolabe or quadrant, applying declination and working out your latitude. Land-based European geographers already knew how to calculate latitude by observation of sun and North Star, but to introduce those methods on board ship took time. Most master mariners and pilots of that era were illiterate, and for them the application of declination to altitude was an insoluble problem. Whether or not D. Henrique held "refresher courses" for pilots in Sagres, the fact is that by 1484, when Diogo Cão discovered the mouth of the Congo, Portuguese ships carried charts with a latitude grid, and Portuguese pilots had built up such a reputation that all organizers of Spanish, English and French voyages of discovery sought to engage one for their ships.

All, that is, except Columbus. But he himself had been trained in the Portuguese service for years before beginning his great voyage.

Enter Columbus

Christopher Columbus was born Cristoforo Columbo, in or near the city of Genoa some time between 25 August and the end of October 1451. He was son and grandson to woolen weavers who had been living in various towns of the Genoese Republic for at least three generations. His long face, tall stature, ruddy complexion, and red hair suggest a considerable share of "barbarian" rather than "Latin" blood, but do not prove anything; and he himself was conscious only of his Genoese origin. There is no more reason to doubt that Christopher Columbus was a Genoa-born Catholic, steadfast in his faith and proud of his native city, than to doubt that Abraham Lincoln was born in Hardin, Kentucky, in 1809, of British stock.

LEFT: Meant to measure celestial declinations, the astrolabe could be used in calculation of latitude. But it was neither sufficiently accurate nor easy to employ to be of great use to mariners.

BELOW: Other sixteenth-century astronomical devices.

Exactly how Columbus looked has been much debated, for the best known portraits of him are dissimilar. This is the oldest picture of him, a wood-cut by Paolo Goivio made many years after his death.

This is not to say that Christopher Columbus was an Italian in the modern sense. The people of proud Genoa, *Genova la Superba*, have always held themselves apart from (and superior to) other Italians. In the *majorat* or entail of his estate that Columbus executed before departing on his Third Voyage to the New World, he charged his heirs "always to work for the honor, welfare and increase of the city of Genoa," and there to maintain a house for some member of the Colombo family, "so that he can live there honorably and have foot and root in that city as a native thereof *... because from it I came and in it I was born.*" And, "being as I was born in Genoa," his executors shall accumulate a fund in the Bank of St. George at Genoa, that "noble and powerful city by the sea."

Every contemporary Spaniard or Portuguese who wrote about Columbus and his discoveries calls him Genoese. Four con-temporary Genoese chroniclers claim him as a compatriot. Every early map on which his nationality is recorded describes him as Genoese or *Ligur*, a citizen of the Ligurian Republic. Nobody in his lifetime, or for three centuries after, had any doubt about his origin or birthplace.

Nevertheless, by presenting far-fetched hypotheses as proved, and innuendoes as facts, by attacking authentic documents as false, and by fabricating others, Columbus has been presented as Castilian, Catalan, Corsican, Majorcan, Portuguese, French, German, English, Irish, Greek, Armenian, Polish, and Russian. And now, American! A Scandinavian writer named Thorwald Brynidsen has "proved" that the dis-coverer was a native North American, a descendant of the eleventh-century Norse colony. He built himself a Viking ship, sailed her to Spain, changed his name to Colón, and set forth to rediscover Vinland!

Enough of these fantasies.

Giovanni Colombo, the Discover's paternal grandfather, was a weaver; his son Domenico, a master weaver, hired a house just inside the Porta dell'Olivella, the east-ern gate of Genoa. About 1445 he married Susanna Fontanarossa, daughter of another local weaver. She brought Domenico a small dowry, and he obtained a respectable municipal appointment as warder of the Olivella gate. In this house, near the gate, in a quarter so rebuilt that the site cannot now be definitely fixed, Christoforo was born in the late summer or early fall of 1451.

Thus Columbus's forty-first birthday fell during his first great voyage of dis-covery. Very likely he did not remember the exact date, since boys and girls then celebrated the feast day of their patron saint rather than their own birthday. On 25 June, the feast of Saint Christopher, young Christoforo would have made a point of attending Mass with his mother, and then would have received a little pocket money and a glass of wine from his father.

The story of Saint Christopher,* familiar to every child in the Middle Ages, made Columbus's baptismal name far more sig-nificant to him than his patronymic. Chris-topher was a great hulk of a pagan who, hearing of Christ, went forth in search of

---

*Recently and regrettably demoted from saintly status by the Vatican.

This house, near the Olivella Gate in Genoa, is traditionally held to be where Columbus was born, but in fact the exact site cannot be established.

Him. A holy hermit said, "Perhaps Our Lord will show Himself to you if you fast and pray." "Fast I cannot," said Christopher, "and how to pray I know not; ask me something easier." So the hermit said, "Knowest thou that river without a bridge which can only be crossed at great peril of drowning?" "I do," said Christopher. "Very well, do thou who are so tall and strong take up thine abode by the hither bank, and assist poor travelers to cross; that will be very agreeable to Our Lord, and mayhap He will show Himself to thee." So Christopher built himself a cabin by the river bank and, with the aid of a tree trunk as a staff, carried wayfarers across on his broad shoulders.

One night the big fellow was asleep in his cabin when he heard a child's voice cry, "Christopher! come and set me across!" Out he came, staff in hand, and took the infant on his shoulders. But as he waded through the river the child's weight increased so that it became almost intolerable, and he had to call forth all his strength to avoid falling and to reach the other bank. "Well now, my little fellow," said he, "thou hast put me in great danger, for thy burden waxed so great that had I borne the

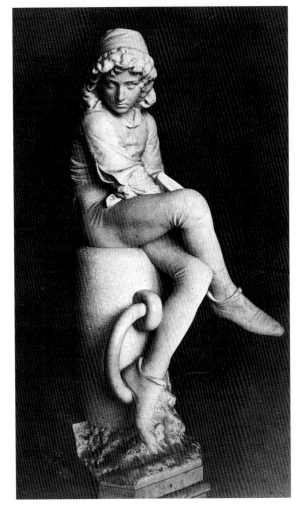

If we do not know how Columbus looked as an adult, it is even less possible to say how he looked as a boy, but that has not deterred artists such as the Genoese sculptor who made this statue of the young Christopher.

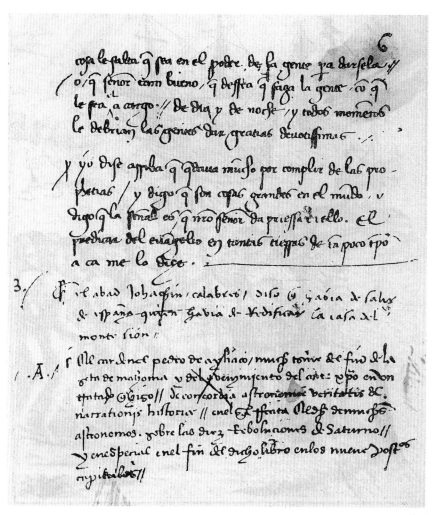

with a courtyard and garden near the Porta Sant' Andrea. His next younger brother, Bartholomew, the future *Adelantado*, was then about two years old. His youngest brother, Giacomo or Diego, seems to have been Christopher's junior by seventeen years. Christopher felt for him the affection that an older brother often does for the baby of the family. He took him on his Second Voyage, and after ascertaining the young man to be an indifferent seaman and a bad administrator, helped him to obtain holy orders and made futile efforts to procure a bishopric for him.

Domenico Colombo, the father of these three boys, was a master clothier (to use the old English term) who owned one or more looms, bought his own wool, sold the finished cloth, and taught apprentice boys their trade. As a citizen of Genoa and member of the local clothiers' gild, he had a respectable position in the middle class. A fairly vivid personality emerges from the dry records. He made promises that he was unable to fulfill, bought goods for which he could not pay, and started unprofitable sidelines such as selling cheese and wine instead of sticking to his loom. Although a poor provider for his family, Domenico

ABOVE: An example of Columbus's handwriting. He wrote in Castilian Spanish, but with some Portuguese spellings. There is no evidence that he wrote Italian.

RIGHT: The Christopher Columbus monument in Genoa, located near a spot where the Admiral may have been born.

whole world on my back, it could have weighed no more than thou." "Marvel or not, Christopher," replied the child, "for thou hast borne upon thy back the whole world and Him who created it. I am the Christ whom thou servest in doing good; and as proof of my words, plant that staff near thy cabin, and tomorrow it shall be covered with flowers and fruit." The saint did as he was bid, and found his staff next day transformed into a beautiful date palm.

This story would certainly have gone home to the boy who became the man we know as Columbus. He conceived it his destiny to carry the word of that Holy Child across the ocean to countries steeped in heathen darkness. Many years elapsed and countless discouragements were surmounted before anyone would afford him means to take up the burden. Once assumed, it often became intolerable, and often he staggered under it; but never did he set it down until his appointed work was done.

In 1455, when Christopher was four years old, his parents removed to a house

must have been a popular and plausible sort of fellow to obtain property on credit and to be appointed on committees of his gild. He was the kind of father who would shut up shop when trade was poor and take the boys fishing; and the sort of wine seller who was his own best customer.

For years the records tell us nothing of the Colombos. By March 1470 Domenico had removed to nearby Savona with his

This almost medieval-looking world map was drawn as late as 1448. It is oriented with north at the bottom.

It is on fragmentary evidence such as the ship shown on the title page of this 1518 book that modern scholars must depend when they try to reconstruct how Columbus's vessels may actually have looked.

history, we may assume that he was a proud and sensitive lad, faithful to his religious duties, following a hereditary calling in order to help support his parents, but eager for adventure, mystically assured of a high mission and a noble destiny.

The absence of Italian in his preserved writings, except for a stray word or phrase, is a great talking point of the *Colón Español* and *Colom Català* sects. The earliest bit of his writing that has been preserved, a postil (marginal note) dated 1481 on one of his books, is in bad Spanish mingled with Portuguese; all his letters, even those to Genoese friends and to the Bank of St. George, are in Spanish. None of the authors to whom he alludes wrote in Italian; the *Divine Comedy*, ever beautiful where Dante describes the sea, apparently he knew not.

Actually the lack of Italian in Columbus's writings is good evidence of his Genoese birth. The Genoese dialect of his day, even more than in ours (when a Genoese speaking it in a trial at Rome around 1910 had to have an Italian interpreter), was very different from Tuscan or classical Italian; possibly even more so than the Venetian and Neapolitan dialects. It was essentially a language of common speech, rarely written. A poor boy of Genoa would not have known Italian, unless he learned it at school. Christopher undoubtedly left home almost if not completely illiterate, and when he finally learned to read and write, used the Castilian language because it was that of his new associates. Many thousands of peasant Italian emigrants have done just that. Arriving in their New World home illiterate, they learn to read and write in English, Spanish, or Portuguese according to the country of their residence, and eventually forget the dialect they were brought up to speak.

A careful analysis of Columbus's writings has been made by the most eminent Spanish philologist of the last hundred years, Ramón Menéndez Pidal. The Discoverer, he reports, did not write Jewish-Spanish or Italian-Spanish, but Portuguese-Spanish. To the end of his life he wrote Castilian with Portuguese spellings, indicating that he spoke Portuguese first. During the decade he lived at Lisbon, Castilian was a widely favored language among

family and looms. He also retailed wine; on 31 October of that year, son Christoforo, "over 19 years of age," acknowledged a debt of 48 Genoese pounds for wines delivered to him and his father. He lived at Savona long enough to make two fast friends in the upper class: – Michele de Cuneo, who accompanied him on the Second Voyage, and Bartolomeo Fieschi, who on the Fourth Voyage shared the famous rescue voyage from Jamaica to Haiti.

Domenico died about 1496, but was not forgotten; for Christopher and his brother Bartholomew named their new capital, Domingo, after the patron saint of their father.

Such are the facts that we have of the life of Christopher Columbus to the age of twenty-two, and of his family. Since this boy was father to the man of recorded

Here, too, he may even have conceived his grand enterprise; for the achievements of a great man are often by the fulfillment of youthful dreams.

Such speculations are for the poet or novelist, not the historian. All we now know and all we shall probably ever know of Columbus's life to the age of twenty-two is that he helped his parents at Genoa and Savona in their respectable trade of weaving woolens, and that he had little or no schooling. Yet his youth was neither so hard nor his life so bitter as to cause him to forsake allegiance to "that noble and powerful city by the sea."

LEFT: Various types of Mediterranean ships of the sixteenth century illustrated in a book published in 1545.

BELOW: An illustration from a book printed in Lubeck in 1537 shows a northern ship that is less evolved than similar vessels in the Mediterranean.

the educated classes of Portugal into which Columbus married; even Camoëns used that language for his sonnets. So an ambitious young man would naturally have chosen the more literary and widely expanded language.

What effect if any did Christopher's residence of some twenty-two years on Genoese territory have on his future career? Genoa was certainly the place to give any active lad a hankering for sea adventure. The Ligurian Republic bathes in the sea, spreads her arms to embrace it, looks southward to a clean horizon. The *libeccio* (southwest wind) blows in fresh from the Mediterranean and gives the terraced hills above the coast sufficient moisture for tilth, vineyard, and pasture. Shipbuilding went on in little coves and harbors all along the shore. Great galleys and carracks were constantly clearing for and arriving from the Aegean, the Levant, and North Africa. Genoa cherished traditions of navigators like the Vivaldi who sought the ocean route to India by way of Africa as early as 1291, and of Malocello, one of the discoverers of the Canaries. Genoa had a noted school of mapmakers who supplied portolan charts to half the Mediterranean, and who helped the Portuguese to chart their new African possessions. One may picture young Christopher looking wistfully out on the harbor from his parents' house while he worked at a loathed trade.

Dyt ys dat högeste vnde öldeste water recht / dat de gemene Kopman vnd Schippers geordinert vnde gemaket hebben tho Wißby / dat sick eynn yder (de thor Seweit vorkeret) hyr na richten mach.

Gedruckt jn der Keyserliken Stadt Lübeck dorch Jurgen Richolff Wanhafftich jn der Mölenstraten. Int jar M. CCCCC. XXXvij.

ABOVE: The sandglass was usually the only timepiece carried on Renaissance ships.

BELOW: It was possible for seamen to work out latitude with the aid of instruments such as this quadrant designed for taking starsights, but more mathematics were involved than the average sailor knew.

Early Years at Sea

Cristoforo grew up in a community where every healthy boy went sailing whenever he could. Fishing trips, out with the evening land breeze to net sardines by the light of flaring torches and race the fleet home at dawn. Maybe a run over to Corsica and back; seeing the points of a high, jagged island shoulder up over the horizon, watching them run together into one island, and the white specks on the shore become houses. You anchor in a strange harbor where the men jabber in a weird dialect, and the girls seem so much more beautiful and outgoing than those of your home town. Most of Genoa's commerce went by sea; and it would have been natural for Domenico to send Cristoforo along the coast in a little lateen-rigged packet to sell his cloth, and buy wool, wine, and cheese.

Coastwise experience is not to be despised. Whoever can cope with a sudden squall off the mountains near home is half prepared to meet a storm at sea.

In a letter to the Spanish Sovereigns written from Hispaniola in January 1495, Columbus describes a trip across the Mediterranean on board a Genoese ship chartered by King René of Anjou for his short war with the king of Aragon. That could have happened between October 1470 and March 1472. His next recorded voyage was in a Genoese ship named *Roxana* in 1474, to help the city's trading factory on Chios defend itself against the Turks. The valuable product of Chios was the lentisk, from which they extracted gum mastic (*Pistacia lenticus*), a base for varnish; and twice on his First Voyage Columbus inaccurately designated a local tree, the gumbo limbo, as the lentisk,

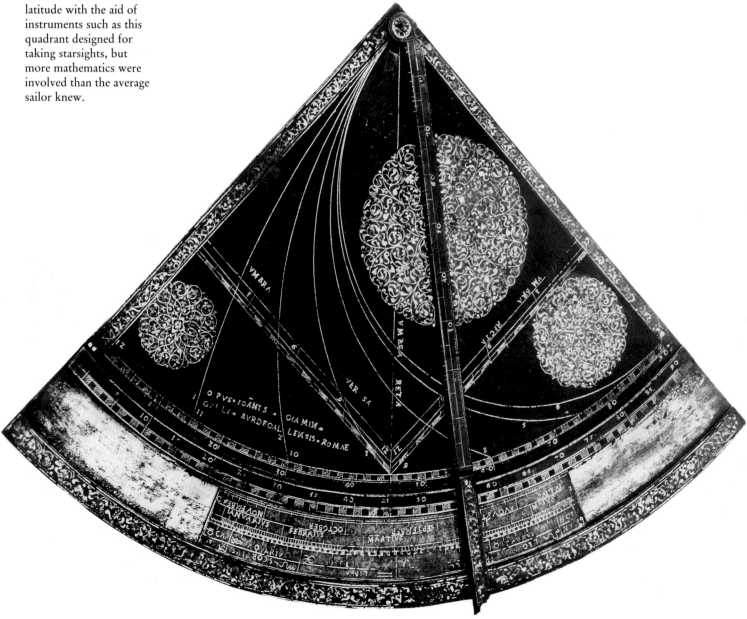

This rich illumination from a Greek codex of the fifteenth century shows the mid-second-century geographer and astronomer Ptolemy in regal garb. Ptolemy's theories continued to dominate geographical thought well into the time of Columbus and encouraged the Admiral to believe the western ocean separating Asia from Europe to be "of no great width."

"which I have seen in the island of Chios." He may have made another voyage to Chios in 1475. On these trips, Christopher learned to "hand, reef and steer," to estimate distances by eye, to make sail, let go and weigh anchors properly, and other elements of seamanship. He learned seamanship the old way, the hard way, and the best way, in the school of experience. As yet illiterate, he could not navigate and thus rate an officer's billet.

Not long after returning from Chios, Columbus joined a fleet that played into the hands of destiny by casting him up on the shore of Portugal. In May 1476, Genoa organized a big convoy to protect a quantity of Chian mastic being shipped to Lisbon, England, and Flanders. One ship, named *Bechalla*, owned by Luis Centurione of Genoa and manned largely by men of Savona, took young Christopher on as foremast hand. On 13 August, off the coast of Portugal near Lagos, the convoy was suddenly attacked by a Franco-Portuguese

A fourteenth-century captain looks at a mariner's compass set on the poopdeck of his ship. It was in this century that the sea compass first came into general use in Europe.

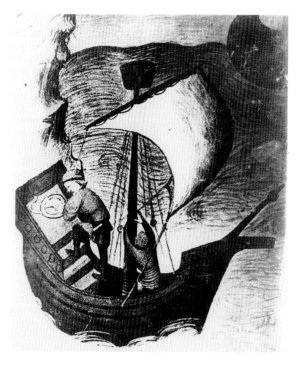

war fleet commanded by a famous naval hero, Guillaume de Casenove. The Genoese proved no easy prey. All day the battle raged, and by nightfall seven ships, including *Bechalla*, had gone down and the surviving vessels were glad to sheer off and seek the nearest friendly port. When *Bechalla* sank, Columbus leaped into the sea, grasped a sweep that floated free, and by pushing it ahead of him and resting when exhausted (for he had been wounded

Compass cards were often arranged to show both directions and the names of the prevailing winds.

in the battle), he managed to reach the shore, over six miles distant. The people of Lagos treated the survivors kindly and passed Columbus on to Lisbon, where someone of the local Genoese colony took him in and cured his wounds. His host may have been his younger brother Bartholomew, who had already established a small chart-making business in Lisbon.

Christopher was in luck to fall on his feet in Portugal. At the age of twenty-five, chance had brought him to the European center for blue-water voyaging and overseas discovery. He was among people who could teach him all he wanted to learn: Portuguese, Castilian, and Latin; mathematics and astronomy for celestial navigation. He already knew all the basic seamanship that a common sailor could pick up.

And he had plenty more on a northern voyage. His son Ferdinand wrote that among his father's notes he found a statement that in February 1477 he sailed a hundred leagues north of Iceland, to which island "which is as big as England, come the English, especially of Bristol, with their merchandise." And he adds that in this particular winter season the sea was not frozen, and the range of tides ran up to fifty feet. This statement has aroused no end of controversy. But the winter of 1476-77 was unusually mild, so that this Portuguese ship could have sailed beyond Iceland to Jan Mayen Land in latitude 70° 50′ N. If, however, Columbus actually did make this voyage, did he land in Iceland and pick up data on the Northmen's explorations of the eleventh century? Son Ferdinand's statement is full of inaccuracies – the latitude he gives for Iceland is more than ten degrees out, and the spring range of tides at Reykjavik is only thirteen feet, not fifty. And even if the ship did land in Iceland, would this young mariner have attended a saga-reading party (in translation) and have heard about Vinland? Not likely. In any case, there was nothing in the Greenland-Vinland story of polar bears, walrus ivory, and white falcons to interest a young seaman already dreaming of an ocean route to the fabulous Indies of gems, spices, and precious metals.

More important to him was something he saw at Galway, going or coming; two boats drifting ashore containing "a man and a woman of extraordinary appear-

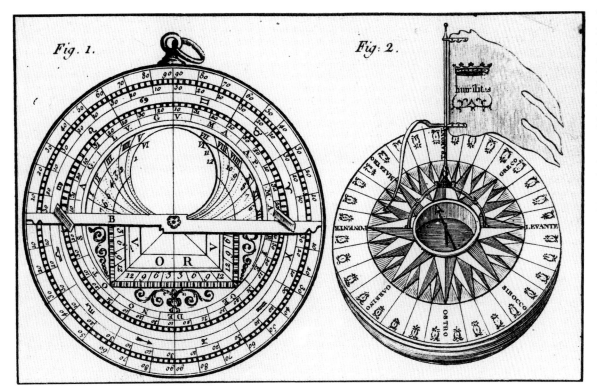

The astrolabe (1) and the mariner's compass were the most advanced navigation instruments of the Renaissance, but both had their flaws. The astrolobe, even if the difficulty of its use could be mastered, was seldom accurate to within a degree, and compasses were subject to variation, a little understood phenomenon.

ance," both dead. These probably were flatfaced Lapps or Finns who had escaped from a sinking ship; but Christopher and the Irish assumed that they were Chinese, "blown across." As for tides, Professor Ruddock of the University of London has a plausible explanation. She found record of a Bristol ship trading in 1481 with the friary of La Rábida where (as we shall see) Columbus became intimate. The Bristolians told the monks about the tremendous tides on the Avon, and they somehow applied this to the Arctic Ocean when Ferdinand, much later, picked up the story of the Iceland voyage.

We find Christopher at sea again in the summer of 1478 as captain of a Portuguese ship which Centurione, his former employer, had chartered to buy sugar in Madeira. This Genoese merchant provided the young captain with so little money that Funchal merchants refused to deliver, and he sailed empty-handed to his old home. Next year Christopher, at twenty-eight years a master mariner, contracted an advantageous marriage with Dona Filipa de Perestrelo e Moniz, daughter of Bartolomeu Perestrelo, hereditary captain of Porto Santo in the Madeira group, and a contemporary of the Infante D. Henrique. The young couple shortly went to live in Porto Santo where their only son, Diego (later the second admiral and viceroy), was

born, and where Dona Filipa's mother placed at Christopher's disposal the charts and journals of her seagoing husband. Not long after the birth of this, their one and only child, the Columbus couple moved to Funchal, Madeira.

In 1481 D. Afonso V died and was succeeded by his son D. João "the Complete Prince." Young (aged 26), energetic, wise and learned, ruthless and ambitious, D. João II equaled any monarch of his age. Just before his accession, a long and fruitless war with Castile had been concluded by the Treaty of Alcáçovas. In this Spain recognized Portugal's exclusive rights to the African coast and islands south of the Canaries, which Spain retained. D. João, who had formerly managed the crown monopoly of the African trade, determined to build a castle or fortified trading factory on the Gold Coast, strong enough to beat off any European rival, and to keep the natives in order. A fleet of eleven vessels was fitted out at Lisbon, soldiers, stonemasons, and other artisans were engaged, and late in 1481 it set sail from Lisbon under the command of Diogo d'Azambuja. On the Gold Coast the men worked hard and well that winter, erecting a great stone castle of medieval design, complete with turrets, moat, chapel, warehouse, and market court; and a garrison was left in charge. São Jorge da Mina (St. George of the Mine),

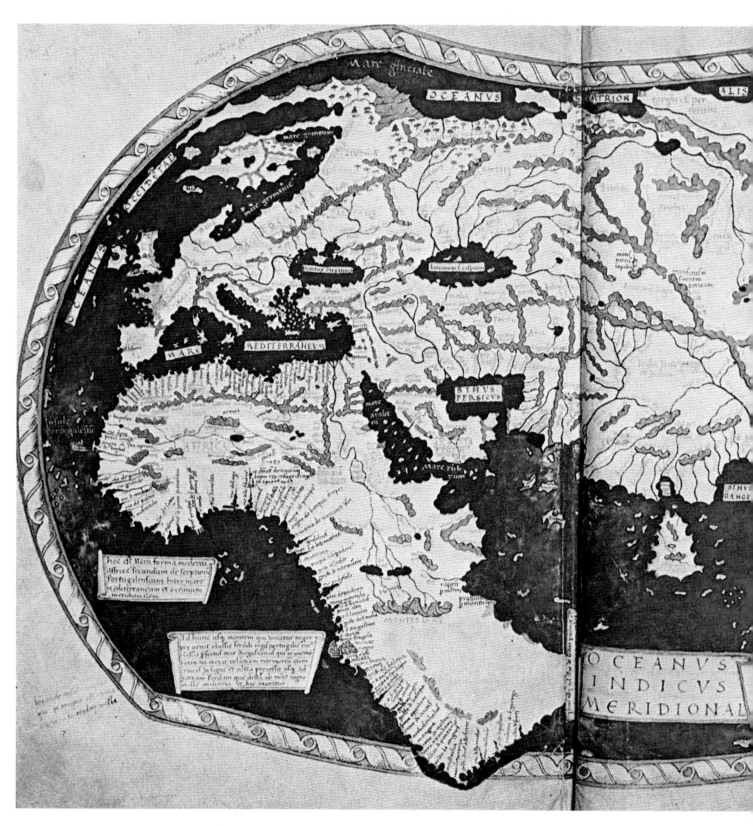

The elaborate detail lavished on the West African coast in this 1489 world map implies the excitement felt by the cartographer about the recent discoveries made by the Portuguese.

as this castle was named, upheld Portuguese sovereignty and protected her trade on the Gold Coast for centuries. The site and the ruins today are called Cape Coast Castle.

Columbus either took part in Azambuja's expedition or, more probably, made a voyage to São Jorge da Mina in 1482-83 or 1483-84, as officer of a trading expedition.

West Africa deeply impressed the young mariner. In the journal of his First Voyage to America he frequently compares people and products of "The Indies" with those of Guinea; he expected to find a *mina* in Hispaniola, and his Third Voyage had particular reference to the supposed latitude of Sierra Leone. The experience of a passage to the Gold Coast and back, in company

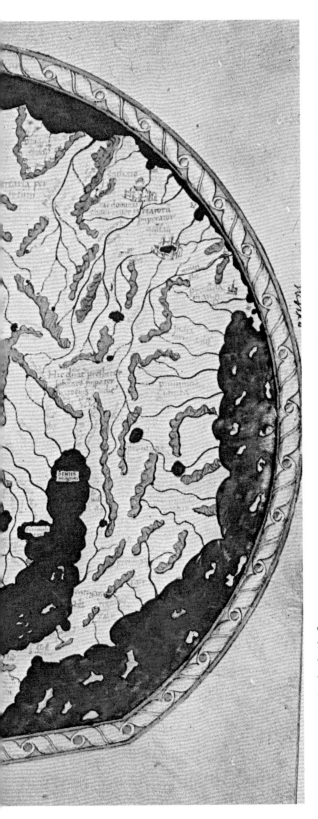

with Portuguese pilots, must greatly have improved his seamanship, although it may be doubted whether it gave him any competence in celestial navigation.

Christovão Colom, as he was called in Portugal, learned many useful things from his Portuguese shipmates, the world's finest mariners of that era: how to handle a caravel in head wind and sea, how to claw off a lee shore, what kind of sea stores to take on a long voyage and how to stow them, and what sort of trading truck is wanted by primitive people. Every voyage that he sailed under the flag of Portugal made it more likely that he would succeed in the great enterprise that was already in his brain. Above all, he learned from the Portuguese confidence that, with a good ship under him and with God's assistance, the boundaries of the known world might be indefinitely enlarged; that the Age of Discovery had only just begun. From his own experiences he had learned that the ancients did not know everything; despite their denials the Torrid Zone was habitable.

By 1484, when he returned from Guinea voyaging, Columbus was ready to make an amazing proposition to the king of Portugal.

TOP: An allegory of the Age of Exploration on a 1584 titlepage.

ABOVE: Columbus, by an anonymous sixteenth-century artist.

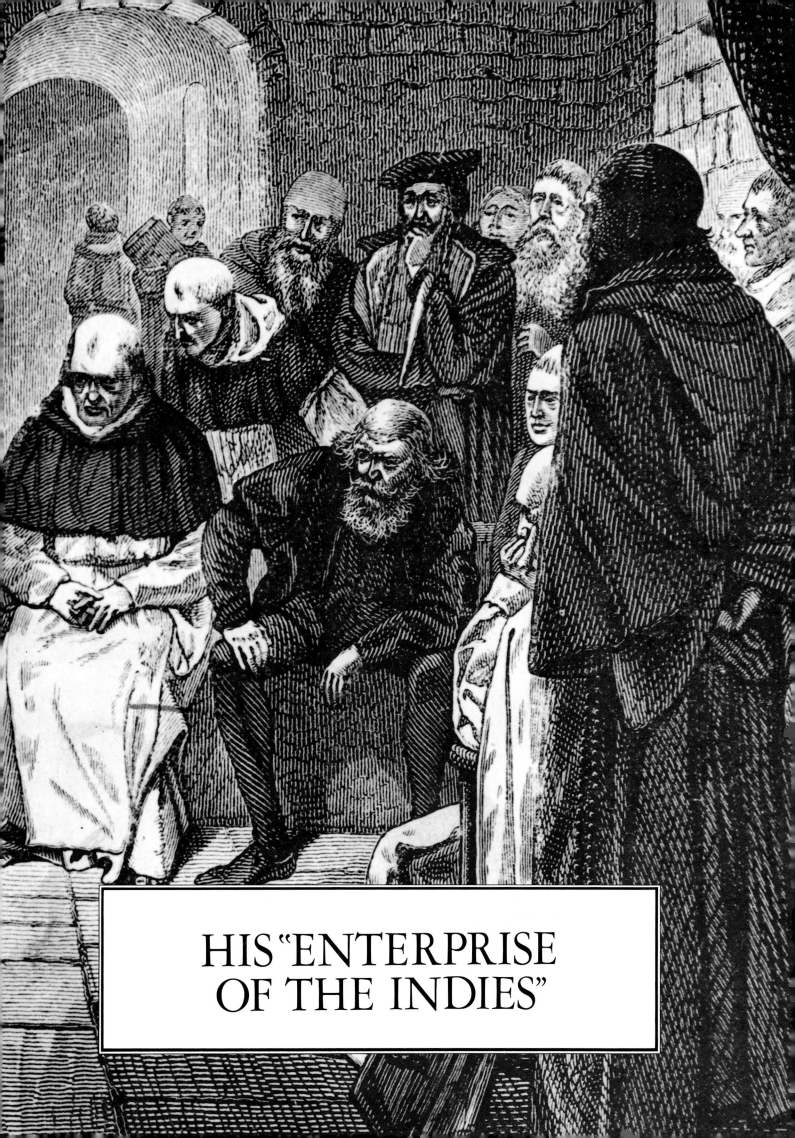

HIS "ENTERPRISE OF THE INDIES"

Columbus's Great Idea

Columbus's "Enterprise of the Indies," *Empresa de las Indias*, as he called it, and to the furthering of which he devoted all his time and energy from about 1483 on, was simple enough. It was to discover a short sea route to the Indies* instead of thrusting along the African coast as the Portuguese were doing. He also hoped to pick up en route some island or archipelago which would be a useful staging area; but the be-all and end-all was to rediscover eastern Asia by sailing west from Europe or Africa. He expected to set up a factory or trading post, like Chios or La Mina, on some island off the Asiatic coast, where European goods could be exchanged for the fragrant and glittering wares of the Orient much more cheaply than by trans-Asia caravans with their endless middlemen and successive mark-ups.

Exactly when Columbus conceived this

PAGES 28-29: Columbus unfolding his plans to the Spanish court at Salamanca, as imagined by a nineteenth-century artist.

BELOW: Columbus as a seventeenth-century artist imagined him.

*"The Indies," as the term was then used in Europe, included China, Japan, the Ryukyus, the Spice Islands, Indonesia, Thailand, and everything between them and India proper.

momentous plan, or had it planted in his brain, is still a mystery. It may have come silently, like the grace of God, or in a rush and tumult of emotional conviction, or from observing, in Lisbon, the painful effort of the Portuguese to approach the Orient by sailing around Africa. All educated men of western Europe knew that the world was a sphere; all observant sailors knew that its surface was curved, from seeing ships hull-down. Columbus never had to argue the rotundity of the earth. When he had learned enough Latin to read ancient and medieval cosmographers, he ascertained that Aristotle was reported to have written that you could cross the Ocean from Spain to the Indies *paucis diebus*, in comparatively few days, and Strabo recorded that certain Greeks or Romans had even tried it but returned empty-handed, "through want of resolution and scarcity of provisions." He picked up from two famous medieval books, Pierre d'Ailly's *Imago Mundi* and Pope Pius II's *Historia Rerum Ubique Gestarum*, numerous guesses about the narrowness of the Ocean; and fortunately we have his own copies of these works, amply underlined, and their margins filled with his postils. He combed the Bible and ancient literature for quotations that might apply to his enterprise, such as Psalm lxxi (or lxxii) 8, "He shall have dominion also from sea to sea, and from river unto the ends of the earth." He cherished the prophecy in Seneca's *Medea* – "An age will come after many years when the Ocean will loose the chains of things, and a huge land lie revealed; when Tethys will disclose new worlds and Thule no more be the ultimate."

Against this passage in Columbus's own copy of Seneca his son Ferdinand wrote this proud annotation:

This prophecy was fulfilled by my father the Admiral, in the year 1492.

The first trace we have of any outside influence on Columbus forming his great idea is the Toscanelli correspondence, his earliest known scholarly backing. Paolo dal Pozzo Toscanelli was a leading Florentine physician in an era when the best astronomers and cosmographers were apt to be medicos, since they alone acquired enough

mathematics to be men of science. Toscanelli had become what nowadays is called a "pen pal" of a canon of Lisbon Cathedral named Fernão Martins, to whom he conveyed the idea that the Ocean between Spain and the Indies was much narrower than anyone else supposed. Martins passed this on to the king, D. Afonso V, who invited the Florentine to develop his views in a letter; and that Toscanelli did. Dated 25 June 1474, a copy of this "Toscanelli Letter" in Columbus's hands became his principal exhibit when arguing for a narrow Atlantic. In brief, it says that Paul the Physician is pleased to hear that the King of Portugal is interested in finding a shorter sea route to "the land of spices" than the one his mariners are seeking via Africa. Quinsay (modern Hangchow), capital of the Chinese province of Mangi, is about 5000 nautical miles due west of Lisbon. An alternate, and shorter, route to the Orient goes by way of Antilia to the "noble island of Cipangu" – Marco Polo's name for Japan, where the temples and royal palaces

are roofed with massy gold. At some time not later than 1481 (Toscanelli died in May 1482), Columbus was shown a copy of this letter, became greatly excited over such exalted backing for his ideas, and wrote to Florence, asking for more. Toscanelli replied by sending a copy of his earlier letter,

ABOVE: An allegory of the eponymous Amerigo Vespucci.

BELOW: If genuine, this 1440 map proves Viking landings in America.

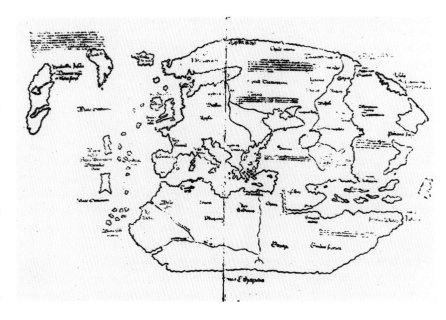

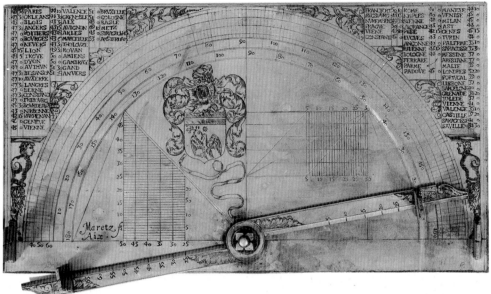

ABOVE: Seventeenth-century navigational instruments were much more refined than those available to Columbus, yet they embodied no new ideas. Instruments of the 1700s would be vastly superior.

TOP RIGHT: *Columbus and His Son at La Rábida*, as painted by Eugène Delacroix in 1838.

RIGHT: The cathedral in Cordova. It was in Cordova that Columbus first met Isabella and explained to her his plan for an "Enterprise of the Indies."

with a chart (long since lost) to illustrate his notion of the Ocean's width, and a covering letter praising the young mariner's "great and noble ambition to pass over to where the spices grow."

By this time Columbus had learned enough Latin to read ancient and medieval authors who speculated on the length of the land and width of the Ocean. The result of his studies was to arrive at an extraordinary perversion of the truth. The distance from the Canaries to Japan via Antilia, which Toscanelli estimated at 3000 nautical miles (and Columbus whittled down to 2400) is actually about 10,000 miles between their respective meridians on latitude 28° N. Toscanelli's Canaries-to-Quinsay route of 5000 miles (reduced by Columbus to 3550) is actually 11,766 nautical miles by air.

How did he arrive at this colossal miscalculation, upon which his great voyage of discovery was based? Through several basic errors: reducing the length of a degree of longitude by one-quarter, stretching Ptolemy's estimate of the length of the Eurasian continent (Cape St. Vincent to eastern Asia) from 180° to 225°, adding another 28° for the discoveries of Marco Polo, plus 30° for his reputed distance from the east coast of China to the east coast of Japan, and saving another nine degrees of westing by starting his Ocean crossing from the outermost Canary Island.* That left only 68° degrees of Ocean to cross before hitting Japan; still too much for Columbus. The medieval calculators used too long a degree of longitude, he argued; he proposed to cross on latitude 28° N where the degree (he thought) measured

---

*Columbus owned a copy (still in the Biblioteca Colombia, Seville) of the 1485 edition of Marco Polo, who placed Japan some 1500 miles east of the coast of China, thus shortening the projected ocean passage.

but 40 nautical miles; thus he would have only 60 × 40 or 2400 miles of open water to cover. In other words, his figures placed Japan in relation to Spain about where the West Indies actually are. That is why those islands were given the name *Las Indias* and their inhabitants called *Indios*, Japan then being reckoned as part of "The Indies." And a Nuremberg geographer named Martin Behaim in the Portuguese service compiled in 1492 a globe that showed a close correlation with what Toscanelli had written.

Columbus's calculations were illogical, but his mind never followed the rules of logic. He *knew* he could make it, and had to put the mileage low in order to attract support.

Another colossal miscalculation of his was the relative proportion of land to water on the globe. Modern measurements divide our planet's surface into 30 per cent land

and 70 per cent water,* but Columbus more than reversed this figure by insisting on the medieval notion (based on 2 Esdras vi. 42, "Six parts has Thou dried up") that water covered less than 15 per cent. Very comforting, if true!

Dealing with Princes

Columbus in 1484, subsequent to his voyage or voyages to Guinea, received a hearing from D. João II. The leading Portuguese historian of this reign, João de Barros, recorded that *Christovão Colom*, "Of Genoese nation, a man expert, eloquent and good Latinist," requested the king to "give him some vessels to go and discover the Isle Cypango by this Western Ocean." D. João referred Christopher to a newly appointed maritime committee. They dismissed him politely but firmly, considering

*Peter J. Herring (ed.), *Deep Oceans*, p. 13. In the Northern Hemisphere the proportion is 40-60; in the Southern, 19-81.

his plan "as vain, simply founded on imagination, or things like that Isle Cypango of Marco Polo." For most learned men at that era regarded *The Book of Ser Marco Polo* as pure fiction, and Cipangu-Japan as a mythical island in a class with Hy-Brasil and Antilia. They felt that the length of the proposed voyage had been fantastically underestimated.

Columbus and D. João parted friends, and were to see each other twice again. But, for the present, there was nothing for him in Lisbon. His wife Dona Filipa had already died. Brother Bartholemew, first convert to the Enterprise of the Indies, then took off for England and France, to promote it.

About the middle of 1485 Columbus and his little son Diego took passage on a merchant ship for Spain and disembarked at a sleepy little seaport called Palos de la Frontera because of its nearness to the Portuguese frontier. Although he probably chose that port to enter Spain for no better reason than having been offered free passage to it by the skipper, it turned out to be as lucky as swimming ashore at Lagos nine years earlier. When his ship rounded the promontory where the Rio Tinto joins the Saltés, Columbus noted the conspicuous buildings of La Rábida, a friary of the Fransiscan order which took more interest in discovery than did any other branch of the church. Franciscan missionaries had been to China around 1320 and others were eager to return. For the present, Columbus, puzzled what to do with little Diego while he tramped about Spain seeking support, remembered that Franciscans often maintained boarding schools in connection with their friaries. Over a quarter-century later, a physician who happenened to be present testified that father and son made the long, dusty walk from Palos to La Rábida, that Columbus asked for bread and a cup of water for the boy, and then got into conversation with Antonio de Marchena, a highly intelligent Franciscan who happened to be visiting. Columbus not only arranged for Diego's admission as a boarder but convinced Marchena, an astronomer of repute, that he "had something"; and Marchena gave him a letter of introduction to the Duke of Medina Sidonia. Columbus called at the ducal castle and was referred to a kinsman, the Count of Medina

Columbus and his sons, Diego and Ferdinand, as an artist in the seventeenth century imagined them.

Celi, who owned a merchant fleet based at Puerto Santa Maria near Cadiz. This nobleman (later promoted duke) declared himself ready to provide Columbus "with three or four well equipped caravels," for he asked no more, but felt that the Enterprise of the Indies was too great for a mere subject to take over; that the Genoese must see the Queen.

As Pierre Chaunu observes, La Rábida became a key to the Christian expansion that flowed from Columbus's voyage, as Palos and the caravels were the keys to immediate success. For Palos, a nursery of Spanish blue-water mariners, lay so close to the Portuguese frontier that an exchange of caraval designs was easy. Without La Rábida and Palos, there would have been no Voyage of Discovery, at least not in 1492.

ABOVE: The Franciscan monastery at La Rábida, where Columbus boarded his son, Diego, and where he received his first encouragement in Spain for his project to sail west to Asia.

LEFT: A painted marble table top with scenes of Columbus's life. In the center picture he explains his theories to a monk at La Rábida.

Columbus now proceeded to the royal city of Cordova. Arriving in January 1486, he missed the Catholic Sovereigns, but tarried to await the Queen's return, and her pleasure.

In the meantime he made a pleasant connection with a pretty peasant girl. At Cordova there was a colony of Genoese, one of them an apothecary, and apothecary shops in those days were informal meeting places for physicians and amateur scientists. Columbus naturally dropped in at his compatriot's shop and there became acquainted with one Diego de Harana, who frequented it. Diego invited him to his house, where he met a twenty-one-year-old cousin of the Haranas, Beatriz Enriquez. She became Columbus's mistress and in 1488 bore him his second son, Ferdinand. The undoubted fact that Columbus never married Beatriz has troubled his more pious biographers, and judging from cer-

tain provisions for her in his will, it troubled his conscience too; but nobody at the time seems to have held it against him. A second marriage with a peasant's daughter would have been unsuitable for one who intended to become a nobleman and an admiral. The Harana family were pleased with the connection; at least two of them later served under Columbus, and the friendship between them and his legitimate descendants continued for two or three generations.

On May Day 1486, almost a year from the time he first set foot in Spain, Columbus was received by the Queen in the Alcazar of Cordova. *Isabel la Católica* (Isabella in English) was one of the ablest European sovereigns in an age of strong kings. She had an intuitive faculty for choosing men, and for timing. Close to Columbus in age, she had blue eyes and auburn hair resembling his, and she shared his religious

The old city walls of Cordova. Once one of Europe's most wealthy and powerful cities, Cordova had already become something of a venerable relic by the time of Columbus.

Ferdinand of Aragon and his queen, Isabella of Castile: details from a painting, *La Virgine dei Re Catolici* (by an unknown artist), now in the Prado.

mysticism. Her marriage with Ferdinand of Aragon had united all "the Spains" excepting Portugal (to whose royal family she was allied) and the remnant of the Moorish caliphate of Cordova, which she had resolved to conquer. Some spark of understanding evidently passed between Columbus and Isabella at their first meeting, and although she turned down his enterprise more than once, he found that he could count on her in the end. On this occasion she appointed a special commission under her confessor Hernando de Talavera to examine the Enterprise of the Indies and recommend whether it should be accepted or rejected.

The most unhappy period in Columbus's life extended over the next six years. He had to sustain a continual battle against prejudice, contumely, and sheer indifference. A proud, sensitive man who *knew* that his project would open fresh paths to wealth and for the advancement of Christ's kingdom, he had to endure clownish witticisms and crackpot jests by ignorant courtiers, to be treated like a beggar; even at times to suffer want. Hardest of all, he learned by experience the meaning of the phrase *cosas de España*, the endemic procrastination of Spaniards. In later years he often alluded bitterly to these experiences and contrasted the enormous wealth and power his discoveries had conferred on

Spain to his own protracted efforts to obtain a fair hearing, and later to secure his just rights.

Even in our day we have known men of great strength of character who felt inspired by God in the pursuit of some ideal goal, who exasperated people who held other views, and were almost impossible to fight against. You can argue your head off against people like that, but they always come up with a fresh argument.

The Talavera commission, meeting at

According to legend, Columbus was subjected to scorn and ridicule when he presented his ideas to the Talavera commission in 1486, but there is no real evidence to support this supposition.

This bas-relief on the Columbus Movement in Genoa is a rather less dramatic, and probably more accurate, version of how the Talavera commission listened to Columbus's proposals than is the scene in the picture on page 37. While it is true that the commissioners did finally turn him down, it took three years of deliberation for them to reach that decision.

Salamanca around Christmastide 1486, could not agree. Its deliberations have been distorted by Washington Irving and other writers into a debate as to whether the world was round or flat. Actually, we know nothing definite about the arguments, but we may be certain that since the commission consisted of men of learning, the sphericity of the earth never came into question. At least one member, Diego de Deza, favored the Great Enterprise; and it was doubtless due to his influence, or Talavera's, that early in 1487 Columbus received a retaining fee of 12,000 maravedis a year, the pay of an able seaman, enough to support a man of his simple tastes.*

Christmas of 1487 passed without any report from the Talavera commission. So, early in 1488, Columbus wrote to D. João II of Portugal, requesting another hearing and asking for a safe-conduct from arrest for his unpaid bills in Lisbon. The King replied promptly and most cordially, urging Columbus to come immediately, and promising protection. The probable reason for this sudden and flattering change of atti-

tude was that Bartholomew Dias, embarked on one more Portuguese attempt to reach the Indies by rounding Africa, had been gone seven months and nothing had yet been heard from him.

For want of funds, Christopher delayed leaving for Lisbon, and before he and his brother Bartholomew (who had remained there) could "do business" with the King, Dias returned. The Columbus brothers were present in December 1488 when his three caravels sailed proudly up the Tagus. Dias had rounded the southernmost cape of Africa – the Cape of Good Hope as the King named it – and sailed well up the east coast, when the men mutinied and forced him to turn back. But he had discovered a sea route to India. That ended D. João's interest in Columbus. Why now invest money in a doubtful West-to-the-Orient project?

Around New Year's 1489 the Columbus brothers decided on a plan of action. Christopher returned to Spain where he still hoped for support from the slow-moving Talavera commission, while Bartholomew sold his chart-making business and embarked on a long journey to persuade some other prince to support the Great Enterprise. Henry VII of England, first to be approached, turned him down flat. Bartholomew then proceeded to France, where Anne de Beaujeu, sister to King Charles VIII, befriended him and employed him to make charts for her at

*To convey the equivalent of Spanish currency of this era, I have tried to state the gold content in U.S. coinage before we went off the gold standards. Thus, 12,000 maravedis equaled about $83 in gold of 1934. Whatever way you figure it, a maravedi was less than a cent in specie value, but its purchasing power was much greater. Twelve maravedis a day were allowed by the crown for feeding each seaman in the navy. A bushel of wheat in 1493 cost 73 maravedis. Sancho Panza's wages from Don Quixote were 26 maravedis a day and found, much better pay than that of Christopher Columbus's gromets.

Fontainbleau. Through her, Bartholomew became friendly with the French king, but never obtained any real prospect of his support.

Success always seemed to be just around the corner, but in 1489 Christopher still had three years to wait before obtaining anything definite. We know very little of how he passed the time, except that he not only sold books but did purposeful reading in works on cosmography that he found in the libraries of monasteries where he received hospitality. Some of these books have been preserved in his son Ferdinand's Biblioteca Colombina at the Cathedral of Seville, and Columbus's marginal notes, especially in Pierre d'Ailly's *Imago Mundi* (3 vols., Louvain, 1480-83) and Pius II's *Historia Rerum Ubique Gestarum* (1477), are most revealing. For instance, these from Pierre d'Ailly:

> The end of the habitable earth toward the Orient and the end of the habitable earth toward the Occident are near enough, and between them is a small sea.

> Between the end of Spain and the beginning of India is no great width.

> An arm of the sea extends between India and Spain.

> India is near Spain.

> Aristotle [says] between the end of Spain and the beginning of India is a small sea navigable in a few days. . . . Esdras [says] six parts [of the globe] are habitable and the seventh is covered with water. Observe that the blessed Ambrose and Austin and many others considered Esdras a prophet.

> The end of Spain and the beginning of India are not far distant but close, and it is evident *that this sea is navigable in a few days with a fair wind*.

The Queen took notice of his return to Castile by giving him an open letter to all local officials, ordering them to feed and lodge him en route to court, which was then being held in a fortified camp outside the Moorish city of Baza, under siege by the Spanish army. There is some indication that Columbus joined the army as a volunteer while waiting for an answer.

Late in 1490 the Talavera commission

issued an unfavorable report. The experts advised the Queen that the West-to-the-Orient project "rested on weak foundations"; that its attainment seemed "uncertain and impossible to any educated person"; that the proposed voyage to Asia would require three years' time, even if the ship returned, which was doubtful; that the Ocean was infinitely larger than Columbus supposed, and much of it unnavigable. And finally, God would never have allowed any uninhabited land of real value to be concealed from His people for so many centuries! But one must admit that most of the commission's arguments were sound. Suppose that no America existed, no ship of that era, however resolute her master and crew, or frugal in provision, could have made a 10,000-mile non-stop voyage from

Portuguese explorer Vasco de Gama enters the Zamorin's Palace in Calcutta in 1498. The brilliance of da Gama's achievement in finding a sea route to India had, however, already been somewhat dimmed by the news of Columbus's discovery of a westward route to the Far East.

Spain to Japan. Magellan's voyage would prove that.

Apparently a complete stand-off. Columbus knew he could do it; the experts were certain he could not. It needed something as powerful as feminine intuition to break the deadlock. The Queen did give Columbus fresh hope. He could apply again, said she, when the war with the Moors was over. He waited almost another year and then decided to leave Spain and join his brother in France. Calling at the La Rábida friary near Palos to pick up son Diego, now about ten years old, he was persuaded by the prior, Father Juan Pérez to give the Queen another chance, and he wrote to her to that effect. She replied by summoning Columbus to court and sent him some money to buy decent clothing and a mule.

Columbus always found more friends and supporters among priests than among laymen. They seemed to understand him better, since his thoughts, deeds, and aspirations were permeated with religious faith. He was more particular than many clergy in saying daily the Divine Office of the church – prime, tierce, sext, nones, and compline; and seldom missed an opportunity to hear Mass. He had a fine presence and an innate dignity that impressed people of whatever estate, and although he never

ABOVE: Vasco da Gama, from a seventeenth-century manuscript.

RIGHT: A map showing the impressive extent of the exploration the Portuguese conducted in Africa and Asia in the years between 1487 and 1557.

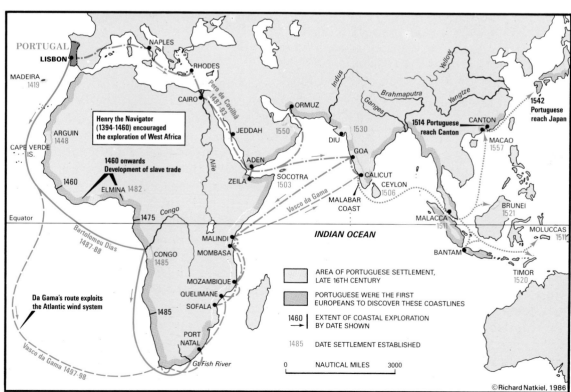

©Richard Natkiel, 1986

spoke perfect hidalgo Castilian, it was not expected that he should as Genoa-born and a former resident of Portugal.

Isabella Takes Him On

At about Christmastime 1491 Columbus again appeared at court, then being held in the fortified camp of Santa Fe during the final siege of Granada. The Royal Council reviewed the findings of a new commission. Although the exact details are not known, it seems probable that the commission, reading the Queen's mind, recommended that Columbus be allowed to try, but the Council rejected it because of the price he asked. For this extraordinary man, despite poverty, delay, and discouragement, had actually raised his demands. In 1485 he had been willing to sail west for Medina Celi on an expense-account basis without any particular honors or emoluments. Now he demanded not only the title of Admiral, but also that he be made

Ferdinand and Isabella recaptured the city of Granada from the Moors in 1492 and there, some months later, formally agreed to Columbus's project. Shown here is Granada's Royal Chapel, where the two monarchs are now buried.

The arms belonging to the city of Granada.

governor and viceroy of any new lands he might discover, that both titles be hereditary in his family, and that he and his heirs be given a 10 per cent cut on the trade. He had suffered so many insults and outrages during his long residence in Spain that – by San Fernando! – he would not glorify Spain for nothing. If the Sovereigns would grant him, contingent on his success, such rank, titles, and property that he and his issue could hold up their heads with the Spanish nobility, well and good; but no more bargaining. Take it, Your Majesties, or leave it.

Leave it they did, in January 1492, immediately after the fall of Granada. Ferdinand and Isabella told him this at an audience which the King, at least, intended to be final. Columbus saddled his mule, packed the saddlebags with his charts and other exhibits, and started for Seville with his faithful friend Juan Pérez, intending to take ship for France and join Bartholomew in a fresh appeal to Charles VIII.

Just as, in Oriental bargaining, a storekeeper will often run after a departing customer to accept his last offer, so it happened here. Luis de Santangel, keeper of King Ferdinand's privy purse, called on the Queen the very day that Columbus left

Santa Fe and urged her to meet Columbus's terms. The expedition, he pointed out, would not cost as much as a week's entertainment of a foreign prince. This Genoese asked for honors and emoluments only in the event of success; and they would be a small price to pay for the discovery of new islands and a western route to the Indies. The Queen jumped at this, her really last chance. She even proposed to pledge her crown jewels for the expenses, but Santangel said that would not be necessary; he would find the funds, and did. A messenger overtook Columbus at a village four miles from Santa Fe, and brought him back.

Although the voyage was now decided upon in principle, there were plenty more *cosas de España* to be endured, and it was not until April 1492 that the contracts between Columbus and the Sovereigns, the Capitulations as they are generally called, were signed and sealed. Therein the Sovereigns, in consideration that Cristóbal Colón (as Columbus was now called in Spain) is setting forth "to discover and acquire certain islands and mainlands in the Ocean Sea," promise him to be Admiral thereof, and viceroy and Governor of lands that he may discover. He shall have 10 per cent of all gold, gems, spices, or other merchandise produced or obtained by trade within those domains, tax free; he shall have the right to invest in one-eighth of any ship going thither; and these offices and emoluments will be enjoyed by his heirs and successors forever. The Sovereigns also issued to him a brief passport in Latin, stating that they were sending him with three caravels "toward the regions of India" (*ad partes Indie*) and three identical letters of introduction, one to the "Grand Khan" (the Chinese emperor) and the other two with a blank space so that the proper title of any other prince could be inserted.

To us, accustomed to the power of Asiatic countries, it seems impossibly naïve for a European to expect to land somewhere on the coast of China or Japan with fewer that one hundred men, and "take over." But Europe was then grossly ignorant of the Far East; the Portuguese had no difficulty in dealing with black kings in Africa, so why should not Columbus do the same thing in Asia? Moreover, the establishment that Columbus had in mind was not what we think of as a colony, but a

Fernad⁹ rex hyſpania

This old wood-block print shows a martial Ferdinand holding the royal arms of Spain in his right hand and the arms of recently-taken Granada in his left.

factoria, feitoria, or factory, long familiar to Europeans. This was something more than a trading post; an extension of sovereignty for commercial purposes. It might be armed, if located in a relatively savage region like São Jorge da Mina on the Gold Coast; or it might be a peaceful extra-territorial settlement such as the Hanseatic League's steelyard in London and the Merchants Adventurers' factory in Amsterdam. The 1492 globe of Martin Behaim, who shared Columbus's geographical ideas, shows an archipelago south of Japan, corresponding to the Ryukyus. Supposing the Ocean had been as narrow as Columbus estimated, and no American barrier, he might have fetched up on an island like Okinawa and there set up an entrepôt between China and the West, both for commerce and conversion. That was what eventually happened at Manila.

Preparing for the First Voyage

Practical details came next. For good reasons, it was decided to fit out the fleet and recruit the men at Palos, the same little

A view of the cramped living space beneath the quarterdeck of the *Santa Maria* (from the official 1929 Spanish reconstruction of the Admiral's flagship).

Illustrating the first page of Columbus's 1493 *Epistola de insulis nuper repertis* is this drawing of a ship by Erhard Reuwich. It is thought by experts to be very similar in its general appearance to the *Santa Maria*.

port in the Niebla district of Andalusia, where Columbus had first set foot in Spain. There he had made friends of the Pinzón family, leading ship-owners and master mariners who had built caravels like those of nearby Portugal, and who enjoyed the confidence of local sailors. Palos, more-over, had committed some municipal mis-demeanor for which the Queen conve-niently fined her two well-equipped caravels. Columbus, with his friend Fray Juan Pérez, made a public appearance in the Church of St. George, Palos, on 23 May 1492, while a notary read the royal order. It so happened that a ship from Galicia, owned and captained by Juan de La Cosa, then lay in port. Columbus chartered her as his flagship, making a fleet of three.

This *Santa Maria*, the most famous of Columbus's ships, left her bones on a reef off Hispaniola, and no picture or model or her has survived; but several conjectural models have been made, and at least three full-size "replicas" have been constructed in Spain. The original *Santa Maria* was probably of about 100 tuns' burthen, which meant that her cargo capacity was 100 tuns (double hogsheads) of wine. Her rig, the conventional one for a *nao*, or ship, called for a mainmast taller than her length; the main yard, as long as the keel, spread an im-mense square sail (the main course), counted on to do most of the driving. Above the main course a short yard spread a tiny main topsail. The foremast, much shorter than the main, carried but one square sail. The mizzen mast, stepped on the high poop, carried a lateen sail, and under the bowsprit hung a square spritsail, which performed rather inefficiently the function of a modern jib.

Here, as near as we can state it after the careful researches of the late Alice Gould and Admiral Julio Guillén y Tato, and of the Admiral's former subordinate Juan Maria Martínez-Hidalgo, is the task organization of Columbus's First Voyage of Discovery. This little fleet with the great destiny had no official name – so at long last let us give it one:

La Armada de India, 1492
Capitán General: Cristóbal Colón

SANTA MARIA, *nao* (ship) of *c.* 100 tuns' bur-then, *c.* 85 feet overall.
Captain: Columbus. Master and owner, Juan de La Cosa. Pilot, Peralonso Niño. *Alguacil* (marshal), Diego de Haran. *Escribano* (scribe, secretary), Rodrigo de Escobedo. Interpreter, Luis de Torres. Surgeon, Juan Sánchez. Seven petty officers, captain's steward and page, 11 able seamen, 10 *grumetes.** Total, 40.

---

*"Gromets," in Elizabethan English; these were either young landsmen who had never been to sea before so not entitled to be called *marineros*, or ship's boys, or apprentice seamen.

PINTA, *caravela redonda* (square-rigged caravel) of *c.* 60 tuns, *c.* 69 feet overall.
Captain: Martín Alonso Pinzón. Owner and able seaman, Cristóbal Quintero. Master, Francisco Martín Pinzón. Pilot, Cristóbal García Sarmiento. Marshal, Juan Reynal. Surgeon, Maestro Diego, Two petty officers, 10 able seamen, 8 gromets. Total, 27.

NIÑA, caravel of *c.* 50 tuns, *c.* 55 feet overall.
Captain: Vicente Yáñez Pinzón. Master and owner, Juan Niño. Pilot, Sancho Ruiz de Gama. Surgeon, Maestre Alonso. Marshal, Diego Lorenzo. Two petty officers, 8 able seamen, 6 gromets. Total, 21.

Allowing for three more people whose names have not been found, the fleet's grand total was about 90 men and boys.

Compared with other recorded task organizations in the era of discovery, this one was exceedingly modest. Only John Cabot's and Verazzano's single-ship expeditions were smaller.

Regarding the crew, two qualities stand out: homogeneity and good health. The only foreigners on board were Columbus, one other Genoese, one Venetian, and one Portuguese; and not one man died at sea – and extraordinary record as we shall see in comparison with later voyages. The only casualties were the men left behind in Haiti. In contrast to later Spanish voyages such as Magellan's and Loaysa's, there were no priests and few "idlers" (as sailors used to call everyone who did no physical work); each captain was allowed but one page or servant.

A Spanish ship in those days had an official name, usually that of a saint, and a nickname which the sailors used; theirs for *Santa Maria* was *La Gallega*, "The

LEFT: A reconstruction of *Santa Maria* made by the Spanish government in 1929 gave the ship a caravel's hull. Most experts today consider this to be incorrect.

BELOW: A view of the 1929 reconstruction of *Santa Maria* just prior to her launching.

This replica of *Niña* was built in Spain and was sailed to Watlings Island in 1962. Though the original *Niña* was a fine sailer, not so the replica, proving once again that we have much to learn about what Columbus's ships were really like.

Galician." One of the two caravels provided by the town of Palos took her name *Santa Clara* from a local saint, but is better known by her nickname *Niña*, so given because she belonged to the Niño family of Palos. *Niña* was Columbus's favorite. She carried him safely home from his First Voyage, took him to western Cuba and back to Spain on the Second, and made another voyage to Hispaniola. At the start she was rigged with three lateen sails like a Portuguese caravel, but in the Canaries Columbus had her rerigged square like her two companions, because square sails are much handier than lateen rig when running before the wind. *Pinta,* also a locally built caravel, was a little larger than *Niña*, and square-rigged from the first. Her real name

we do not know; *Pinta* was probably derived from a former owner named Pinto. She was a smart sailer; the New World was first sighted from her deck, and she made first home.

All three were fastened mostly with wooden trunnels or pins such as one sees in the frames of colonial houses; iron fastenings were used only in key spots. They carried inside stone ballast. Their sides were painted gay colors above the waterline and, below it, payed with pitch to discourage barnacles and teredos (ship worms). Crosses and heraldic devices were emblazoned on the sails, and the ships carried a variety of brightly colored flags to be flown on entering and leaving port. Queen Isabella's royal ensign, quartering the castles and lions of Castile and Leon, streamed from the main truck, and on the foremast flew the banner of the expedition: a green cross on a white field with a crown on each arm – a concession to Aragon. All three vessels carried a little crude artillery, to repel pirates or other unwelcome boarders, but they were in no way combatant ships, and carried neither soldiers nor gunners.

Columbus as a foreigner could never have recruited officers and men without the enthusiastic support of the three leading shipping families of Palos – Pinzón, Niño, and Quintero. Martín Alonso Pinzón commanded *Pinta* and took his younger brother Francisco along as master, a rank that corresponds roughly to the modern first mate. Another brother, Vicente Yáñez Pinzón, commanded *Niña*, and Vicente Yáñez became a discoverer in his own right. *Niña*'s master-owner was Juan Niño; his brother Peralonso Niño, who piloted *Santa Maria*, also became an explorer. La Cosa remained on board the flagship as master. Each vessel had a pilot, a very important rank as he was supposed to take charge of deep-sea navigation.* Each carried a surgeon. Among the "idlers" were certain specialists – Luis de Torres, a converted Jew who knew Arabic (Columbus thought that this would enable him to converse with Chinese and Japanese); Rodrigo Sánchez, the royal comptroller, whose main duty was to see that the crown got its share of any gold acquired; and Pedro Gutiérrez, formerly butler of the king's dais, who shipped as chief steward. Diego de Harana, a cousin of Columbus's mistress, served as *alguacil*, marshal of the fleet, corresponding to the old naval rating of master-at-arms.

Almost all the enlisted men were from the Niebla or the cities of Andulasia: Seville, Cordova, and Jerez de la Frontera. Each seaman received about the equivalent of $7.00 in gold per month, the petty officers twice that, and the boys about $4.60.

It is not true that an Englishman and an Irishman were on board, but there is foundation for the jailbird tradition. Three local lads who had been sentenced to life imprisonment for helping a condemned

This reconstruction of Columbus's cabin on board *Santa Maria* is probably dimensionally accurate, even if the furnishings are more-or-less conjectural.

murderer to break jail were set free in return for shipping with Columbus; they turned out to be trustworthy and sailed with him on later voyages, as did a considerable number of the others. In general, Columbus's crews were made up of sound, capable men and boys from the locality, with members of three leading families in key positions. Encouraged by an ancient pilot who was sure he had just missed the Indies on a Portuguese voyage westward forty years earlier, these *hombres* overcame a mariner's natural conservatism in the hope of winning glory, gold, and adventure. Those who survived won plenty of the first two, and all shared in one of the greatest adventures of all time – Columbus's First Voyage.

---

*On Spanish ships the order of precedence was captain, pilot, *escribano* (secretary or scribe), and master.

COLUMBUS'S FIRST VOYAGE OF DISCOVERY

August–October 1492

Columbus the Man

Although there exists no contemporary portrait of Christopher Columbus, we are fortunate to have descriptions of his appearance, personality, and character from several men who knew him: his son Ferdinand, who lived with him many years, Oviedo the official historian of the Indies, who witnessed his triumphal return in 1493, and Bishop Las Casas, who met him in 1500 in Hispaniola, and whose father and uncle had been Columbus's shipmates. All three agree that the Admiral was more than middling tall, long-visaged, blue-eyed, with bright red hair which turned gray early; impressive in port and contenance, exuding authority, "worthy of all reverence." Usually pleasant and affable, he became irascible when crossed; and when moved to rebuke sailors, instead of culling obscenities from the choice assortment of seagoing profanity, he uttered no other oath than "By San Fernanado!" and no reprimand except "May God take you!" Persistent to the point of stubbornness, and so confident of being right that Las Casas said he seemed to know the world as if it were his own chamber, Columbus believed that God willed him to discover this short route to the Indies, therefore he must succeed; anything else discovered en route should be considered a divine gift to him and to Spain. He daily read the Divine Office like a priest, observed faithfully all church festivals, cultivated the company of ecclesiastics, headed every letter with a little cross, and often concluded with the prayer:

Jesus et Maria   Jesus and Mary
Sint nobis in via   Be with us on the way.

Confident of being God's instrument, Columbus met the hardships of the sea with stoic endurance. Yet he also had a keen business sense, and planned to establish solidly his rank, titles, and fortune for generations to come. To maintain communication with the Catholic Sovereigns, he saw to it that one or both sons became pages at court, to defend his interests. It is rare that in the twentieth century we can find any descendant of a sixteenth-century discoverer, but Columbus's descendants through his son D. Diego are now numerous and include people of high rank such as the Dukes of Alba and of Veragua.

Columbus's character, tempered in the fire of adversity, did not come out pure steel. A proud and sensitive man, he never forgot the jeers of witless coutiers at his enterprise; and too often, after his triumphal return, he would say, "What a fool you were not to believe me!" Or, "I did it, despite your bad advice!" Thus he got men's backs up, and they did all they could to pull him down, or otherwise bedevil him. They succeeded only too well.

But in this bright August of 1492 his fortunes were at young flood, and that tide in his affairs carried him to a New World.

From Palos to San Salvador

The fleet was ready for sea on 2 August 1492. Every man and boy confessed his sins, received absolution, and received communion at the Church of St. George in Palos. The Captain General (as we should

PAGES 48-49: A fresco in Genoa's Castello di Albertia shows *Santa Maria* (1) and *Niña* as they depart Palos in 1492. The rendering of *Santa Maria* could be fairly accurate, save for too-large poopdeck, spritsail and topsail, but both *Niña's* hull and rigging probably are shown incorrectly.

BELOW: Columbus, as he is portrayed in the Town Hall in Genoa.

call Columbus at this juncture) went on board *Santa Maria* in the small hours of Friday the third, and at break of day made signal to get under way. Before the sun rose, all three vessels were floating down the Rio Tinto on the morning ebb, with sails hanging limp from their yards, the men pulling on long ash sweeps to maintain steerageway. As they swung into the Saltés and passed La Rábida close aboard, they could hear the friars chanting the ancient hymn *Iam lucis orto sidere* with its haunting refrain, *Et nunc et in perpetuum*, "Evermore and evermore."

This fleet of high promise, destined radically to affect world history, sailed parallel to a very different fleet of misery and woe. On the very same tide there dropped down the Saltés the last vessel carrying the Jews whom Ferdinand and Isabella had expelled from Spain; 2 August was their deadline; anyone who remained thereafter was to be executed unless he embraced Christianity. Thousands of pitiful refugees, carrying what few household goods they could stow in the crowded ships, were bound for the more tolerant

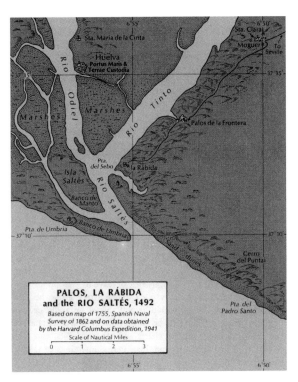

A map of Palos and its environs.

lands of Islam, or for the Netherlands, the only Christian country which would receive them. Columbus has left no word of pity for this persecuted people; he even expressed the wish to exclude them from the

The remains of a small arch in Palos built in commemoration of The First Voyage.

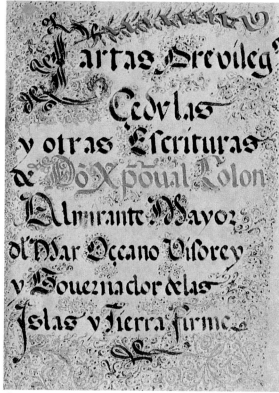

ABOVE: Fanciful scene of Columbus departing from Palos.

BELOW: The Columbus Monument on Punta del Cebo in Spain.

lands he discovered. But, had there been a new prophet of Israel, he might have pointed out the Columbian fleet to his wretched compatriots on that August morning, as the ships which in due time would lead the way to a new life for the Jewish exiles.

The Captain General's simple, seaman-like plan for the voyage ensured its success. He would carefully avoid the boisterous head winds, monstrous seas, and dark un-bridled waters of the North Atlantic which had already baffled Portuguese would-be discoverers thrusting westward. Instead,

he would run south before the northerlies prevailing off Spain and North Africa to the Canary Islands and there make, as it were, a right-angle turn. For he had observed on his African voyages that winter winds in the latitude of the Canaries blew from the east. Moreover, the mean latitude of the Canaries, 28° N, he believed would cut Japan, and also pass the spot where several maps of the period located the mythical isle of Antilia, which would make a good break. Thus, he proposed to reach the Indies by the same traditional "latitude sailing" practised by northern seamen even before the invention of the compass.

On the first leg of the voyage, *Pinta*'s rudder jumped its gudgeons, so Columbus decided to send her into Las Palmas for repairs while *Santa Maria* and *Niña* went to Gomera, westernmost of the conquered Canary Islands. There he sent men ashore to fill water casks, buy breadstuffs and cheese, and salt down native beef. He then sailed to Las Palmas to superintend *Pinta*'s repairs and with her returned to Gomera. By 2 September all three ships were anchored off San Sebastián, the port of Gomera. Columbus there met Doña Beatriz de Peraza y Bobadilla, widow of the former captain of the island, a beautiful

OPPOSITE TOP RIGHT: The frontispiece of the Book of Privileges granted to Columbus on his return from his First Voyage.

ABOVE: The courtyard of the house in which Columbus stayed while he was in Las Palmas in the Canaries during the initial phase of the First Voyage.

LEFT: Pico de Teide on Tenerife, a Canaries landmark familiar to Columbus and all other sailors navigating in those waters.

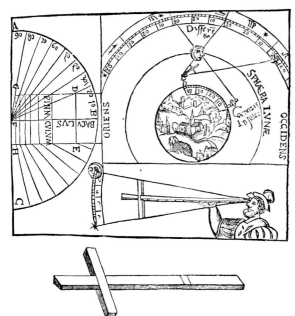

lady still under thirty. He is said by a ship-mate to have fallen deeply in love with her; nonetheless, he did not tarry. Additional ship's stores were quickly hoisted on board and struck below, and on 6 September 1492 the fleet weighed anchor for the last time in the Old World. It had still another island to pass, lofty Ferro, or Hierro. Owing to calms and variables, Ferro and the 12,000-foot peak of Tenerife were in sight until the ninth, but by nightfall that day every trace of land had sunk below the eastern horizon, and the three vessels were alone on an uncharted ocean. The Captain General himself gave out the course: "West; nothing to the north, nothing to the south."

How were those vessels navigated? Celestial navigation was then in its infancy, but rough estimates of latitude could be made from the height of the North Star above the horizon and its relation to the two outer stars (the Guards) of the Little

RIGHT: More primitive than the astrolabe or quadrant was a simple device called a cross-staff, also used for finding declinations of heavenly bodies and, thence, latitude. It was probably grossly inaccurate.

BELOW: Early Italian navigator Flavio Giova demonstrating the use of the marine compass.

Bear, or Little Dipper. A meridian altitude of the sun, corrected by the sun's declination, for which tables had long been provided, also produced latitude. But the instruments of observation – a wood or brass quadrant and the seaman's astrolabe – were so crude, and the movement of a ship threw them off to such an extent, that most navigators took their latitude sights ashore. Columbus relied almost completely on "dead reckoning," which means plotting your course and position on a chart from the three elements of direction, time, and speed.

The direction he had from one or more compasses, which were similar to the dry-card type used in small craft until recently. His had a circular card graduated to the 32 points (N, N by E, NNE by N, NE, and so on), with a lodestone under the north point. It was mounted on a pin and enclosed in a binnacle with gimbals so it could swing freely with the motion of the ship. Columbus's standard compass was mounted on the poop deck under observation of the officer of the watch. The helmsman, who steered with a heavy tiller attached directly to the rudder head, operated from the main deck below, and could see very little ahead. *Santa Maria* may have had another compass for him to steer by, but in the two caravels he was conned by the officer of the deck through a hatch, and kept his course steady by the feel of the helm. On a sailing vessel, you can do that; it would be impossible in a power craft.

Time on the vessels of that day was

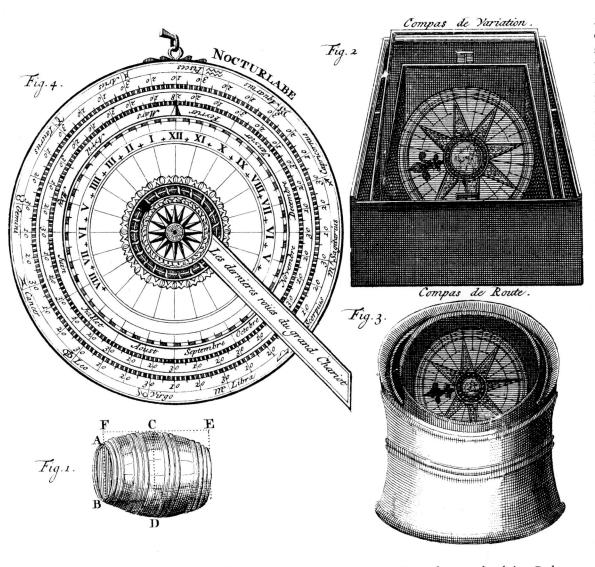

Fig. 4.

NOCTURLABE

Les dernières roües du grand Chariot

Fig. 1.

Compas de Variation.

Fig. 2.

Compas de Route.

Fig. 3.

At top right is a variation compass, used to find the sun's azimuth at dawn, which should be true east. Below it, an ordinary steering compass. To the left, a nocturnal, used for determining the time at night by plotting the movements of various stars. The steering compass apart, Columbus had no such instruments with him on the First Voyage.

measured by a half-hour glass which hung from a beam, so the sand could flow freely from the upper to the lower half. As soon as all the sand had come down a ship's boy turned the glass, and the officer on deck recorded it by making a stroke on a slate. Eight glasses made a watch; the modern ship's bells were originally the means of marking the glasses. This half-hour-glass time could be corrected daily in fair weather, since local noon came when the sun bore due south. Columbus did this every week or so.

Speed long remained the most variable of these three elements. Columbus had no chip log or other method of measuring the speed of his vessels. He or the officer of the watch merely estimated it. Captain J. W. McElroy, by carefully checking Columbus's Journal of his First Voyage, ascertained that he made an average 9 per cent overestimate of distance. This did not prevent his finding the way home, because the mistake was constant, and time and course were correct. It only resulted in Columbus's placing the islands of his discovery further west than they really were.

Even after making the proper reduction for this overestimate, the speed of Colum-

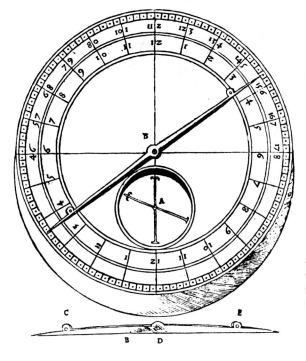

A variation compass card of 1557 showing degrees of bearing in two different scales.

since 1492 have been more in comfort than in speed. Square-riggers of around 1500 actually could sail closer on the wind than their descendants of 1900, because they had much less standing rigging to prevent the yards' being braced sharp up; the mainmast, a stout and not very tall tree, needed much less support than the masts of later centuries.

One reason Columbus always wanted two or more vessels was to have someone

Frigate birds: welcome sights to mariners at sea, as they often indicated that land was nearby.

bus's vessels is surprising. Ships of that day were expected to make 3 to 5 knots in a light breeze, up to 9½ in a strong, fair gale, and at times to be capable of 12 knots. In October 1492 for five consecutive days, the Columbus fleet made an average of 142 miles per day, and the best day's run, 182 miles, averaged almost 8 knots. On the homeward passage, in February 1493, *Niña* and *Pinta* covered 198 miles one day, and at times hit it up to 11 knots. Any yachtsman today would be proud to make such records. Improvements in sailing vessels

The best-known portrait of Columbus (though not necessarily the most accurate) is the one painted by Ridolfo Bigordi, the son of Ghirlandaio, many years after the death of the Admiral.

to rescue survivors in case of sinking. But he made an unusual record for that era by never losing a ship at sea, unless we count the *Santa Maria*'s grounding without loss of life. Comforts and conveniences were almost totally lacking. Cooking was done over a bed of sand in a wooden firebox protected from the wind by a hood, and tucked under the forecastle. The diet, a monotonous one of salt meat, hardtack, lentils and beans, was washed down by red wine, and when that gave out, by water which often went bad in the casks. Only the captains had cabins with bunks; others slept where they could, in their clothes.

On 9 September 1492, the day he dropped the last land below the horizon, Columbus decided to keep a true reckoning of the course for his own use, and a false one to give out to his people so that they would not be frightened at sailing so far from land. But, owing to his overestimate

"Allegorical" is the only word for this old engraving showing the Admiral, fully armed, surrounded by Neptune, sirens, mermen, whales and nameless monsters.

CHRISTOPH. COLVMB.

A crude precursor of the barometer was the weather glass, which operated on the same general principle. The mercury barometer was not used at sea until the eighteenth century.

of speed, the "false" reckoning was more nearly correct than the "true!"

During the first ten days (9 to 18 September), the easterly trade wind blew steadily, and the fleet made 1163 nautical miles westward. This was the honeymoon of the voyage. *Que era plazer grande el gusto de las mañanas* – "What a delight was the savor of the mornings!" – wrote Columbus in his Journal. That entry speaks to the heart of anyone who has sailed in the trades. It recalls the dawn, kindling both clouds and sails rose-color, the smell of dew drying on a wooden deck, and (a pleasure Columbus never knew) the first cup of coffee. This feeling is beautifully expressed by my old friend Dr. Frederick Fraley in his poem "The Morning Watch:"

> Wide waste of waters, dim receding stars,
> The breeze of dawn that barely fills the
>   sails. . . .
> Creak of the rigging, gently furrowed
>   wave
> Under the bows that answer to the swell,
> Set sails, wet deck, breath of the salty air
> And clear resounding stroke of brazen
>   bell.
> "Our little life is rounded with a sleep."
> Strangers and sojourners we are with Thee,
> But, we who sail the reaches of the deep
> Feel its might, know its serenity,
> Look for the sun in measured course to
>   keep
> Appointment with the morning watch at
>   sea.

Succinctly is the beauty of sailing expressed in a stanza (i. 19) of Camoëns' *Lusiads:*

Já no largo Oceano navegavam
As inquietas ondas apartando;
Os ventos brandamente respiravam,
Das naos as velas concavas inchando:
Da branca escuma os mares se mostravam . . .
"Now in broad ocean navigating / the restless waves parting, / the winds softly blowing, / concave sails filling, / the white foam of their waves following. . . ."

Since Columbus's ships were sailing near the northern limit of the northeast trades, where the wind first strikes the water, he found a smooth sea; and the air (he remarked in his Journal), was "like April in Andalusia, the only thing wanting was to hear the song of the nightingale." But there were plenty of other birds following the ships: the little Mother Carey's chickens dabbling for plankton in the bow waves and the wake; the boatswain bird, so called (as old seamen used to say) because it carries a marlinspike in its tail; the man-of-war or frigate bird, "thou ship of the air that never furl'st thy sails," as Walt Whitman wrote; and when the fleet passed beyond the range of these birds, big Jaeger gulls gave it a call.

On 16 September the fleet first entered a field of sargassum (gulf-weed) and found that it was no hindrance to navigation. "Saw plenty weed" became an almost daily notation in Columbus's Journal. The gulf-weed bothered him much less than observing a westerly variation of the compass, for in European waters the variation at this era was easterly.

Ten days out from Ferro, the fleet temporarily ran into an area of variable winds and rain. It had reached the point on Columbus's chart where the fabled island of Antilia should have been, and all hands expected to sight land. The Captain General ordered the deep-sea lead to be hove, and spliced together his two 100-fathom lines for that purpose. Naturally he found no bottom – the ocean there is about 2300 fathom deep! Ordinary seamen who, on the tenth day of the northeast trades, were beginning to wonder whether they would ever beat back home, were cheered by the change of wind. They were never bothered by fear of "falling off the edge of the world" – that is just one of the many old wives' tales about this voyage.

Only 234 miles were made good during the next five days. During this spell of

A nineteenth-century print shows Columbus consulting his compass. In fact, in 1492 the compass was probably too valuable to have been kept on deck.

moderate weather it was easy to converse from ship to ship. In the middle of one of the colloquies, a seaman of *Pinta* gave the "Land Ho!" and everyone thought he saw an island against the setting sun. Columbus fell on his knees to thank God, ordered *Gloria in Excelsis Deo* to be sung by all, and set a course for the island. But at dawn no island was visible, for none was there. A cloudbank above the western horizon, a common phenomenon at sea, had deceived all hands. Columbus refused to beat about looking for this island because, he said, "His object was to reach the Indies, and if he had delayed, it would not have made sense."

The trade wind now returned moderately, and during the six days, 26 September to 1 October, the fleet made only 382 miles. Under these circumstances the people began to mutter and grumble. Three weeks was probably more than they had ever been beyond the sight of land. They were probably all getting on each other's nerves, as happens even nowadays on a long voyage to a known destination. Grievances, real or imaginary, were blown up; cliques were formed; fist fights had to be broken up by the alguacil, the master-at-arms. Every minute Spain grew further away, and what lay ahead? Probably nothing, except in the eye of that cursed Genoese. Let's make him turn back, or throw him overboard!

On the first day of October the wind increased, rain fell in torrents, replenishing the water casks, and in five days (2 to 6 October) the fleet made 710 miles. On the sixth, when they had passed longitude 65° W and actually lay directly north of Puerto Rico, Martín Alonso Pinzón shot his agile *Pinta* under the flagship's stern and shouted, "Alter course, sir, to southwest by west . . . Japan!" Columbus did not understand whether Martín Alonso meant that he thought they had missed Japan and should steer southwest by west for China, or that Japan lay in that direction; but he knew and Pinzón knew that the fleet had sailed more than the 2400 miles which, according to their calculations, lay between the Canaries and Japan. Naturally Columbus was uneasy, but he held to the west course magnetic, which, owing to the variation for which he did not allow, was about west by south, true.

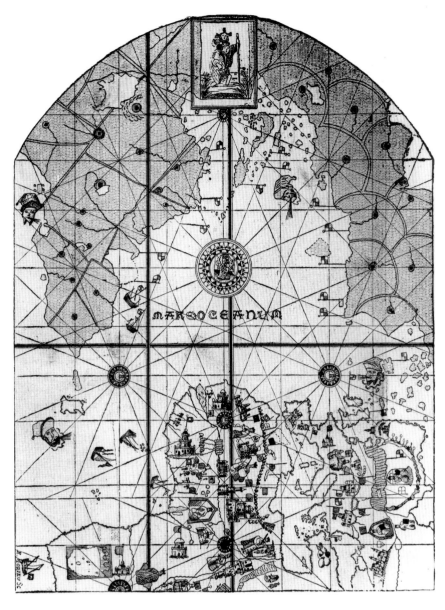

On 7 October, when *Niña* made another false landfall, great flocks of birds passed over the ships, flying west-southwest; this was the autumn migration from eastern North America to the West Indies. Columbus decided that he had better follow Pinzón and the birds rather than his chart, and changed course accordingly that very evening. A very good guess, for this was his shortest route to the nearest land. Every night the men were heartened by seeing against the moon (full on 5 October) flocks of birds flying their way. But mutiny once more reared its ugly head. Even by Columbus's phony reckoning which he gave out, they had sailed much further west than anyone had expected. Enough of this nonsense, sailing west to nowhere; let the Captain General turn back or else –! Columbus, says the record, "cheered them as best he could, holding out good hope of the advantages they might gain; and he added,

A drawing made from a 1500 map by Juan de la Cosa, who accompanied Columbus on the First Voyage. The original map is shown on the following page.

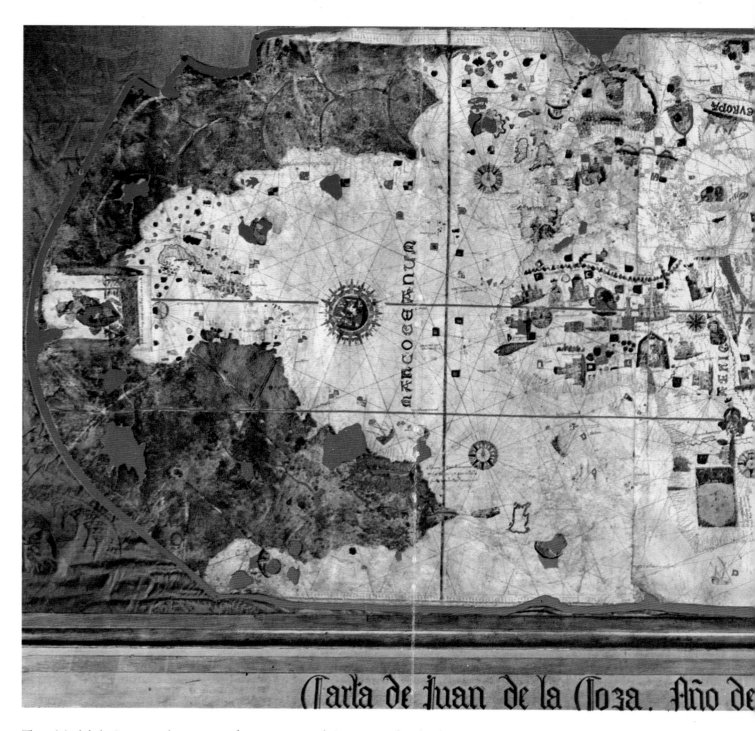

Carta de Juan de la Cosa. Año de

The original de la Cosa map (of which the drawing on page 59 is a detail). It was the first map ever to show the New World.

it was useless to complain, *since he had come to go to the Indies, and so had to continue until he found them, with the help of Our Lord.*"

How typical of Columbus's determination! Yet even he, conscious of divine guidance, could not have kept on indefinitely without the support of his captains and officers. According to one account, Martín Alonso Pinzón cheered him by shouting, *Adelante! Adelante!* which the poet Joaquin Miller translated, "Sail on! Sail on!" But, according to Oviedo, one of the earliest historians who talked with the participants, it was Columbus who per-

suaded the Pinzóns to sail on, with the promise that if land was not found within three days he would turn back. This promise was made on 9 October. Next day the trade wind blew fresher, sending the fleet along at 7 knots, and on the 10th the fleet made a record day's run. On the 11th the wind continued to blow hard, with a heavy following sea. Now signs of land, such as branches of trees with green leaves and even flowers, became so frequent that the people were content with their commander's decision, and the mutinous mutterings died out in keen anticipation of making a landfall in the Indies.

As the sun set under a clear horizon 11 October, the northeast trade breezed up to gale force, and the three ships tore along at 9 knots. Columbus refused to shorten sail, signaled everyone to keep a particularly sharp watch, and offered extra rewards for first landfall in addition to the year's pay promised by the Sovereigns. That night of destiny was clear and beautiful with a late-rising moon, but the sea was the roughest of the entire passage. The men were tense and expectant, the officers testy and anxious, Columbus serene in the confidence that presently God would reveal to him the promised Indies.

At 10:00 p.m., an hour before moonrise, Columbus and a seaman, also simultaneously, thought they saw a light "like a little wax candle rising and falling." Others said they saw it too, but most did not; and after a few minutes it disappeared. Volumes have been written to explain what this light was or might have been. It may well have been a mere illusion created by over-tense watchfulness. But Mrs. Ruth Malvin, a long-time resident of San Salvador, believes it to have been a bonfire lighted by natives living on cliffs or hills on the windward side, to keep sand flies out of their cabins; and this is the best rational ex-

Grahams Harbor on San Salvador (Watlings) Island. The tradition that Columbus made his first landing in the New World on Watlings was challenged in 1986 by a team of *National Geographic* researchers who claim the actual site to be Samaná Cay, 65 miles southeast.

planation yet made. She had fires lighted on High Cay and other places, and when some 28 miles out to sea could see light "rising and falling" just as Columbus said.

The little light does not cause Columbus to alter his course. His ships rush on, pitching, rolling, and throwing spray, white foam at their bows and wakes reflecting the moon. *Pinta* is perhaps half a mile in the lead, *Santa Maria* on her port quarter, *Niña* on the other side. Now one, now another forges ahead. With the fourth glass of the night watch, the last sands are running out of an era that began with the dawn of history. Not since the birth of Christ has there been a night so full of meaning for the human race.

At 2:00 a.m. 12 October, Rodrigo de Triana, lookout on *Pinta*, sees something like a white cliff shining in the moonlight and sings out, *Tierra! tierra!* "Land! land!" Captain Pinzón verifies the landfall, fires a gun as agreed, and shortens sail to allow the flagship to catch up. As *Santa Maria* approaches, Columbus shouts across the rushing waters, "Señor Martín Alonso, you *did* find land! Five thousand maravedis for you as a bonus!"

Land it was this time; gray clay cliffs, white in the moonlight, on the windward

ABOVE: Columbus, as an artist imagines him, hearing the lookout's electrifying cry of "Tierra! tierra!"

RIGHT: An aerial view of the coast of San Salvador.

OPPOSITE TOP: Here, an artist has Columbus making his historic landing in a storm from a seventeenth-century ship.

OPPOSITE BELOW: In a woodcut made in 1493 Columbus's landing is observed by Ferdinand from across the sea.

side of a little island of the Bahama group. The fleet would have crashed had it held course, but these men were no fools to pile up on a lee shore. Columbus ordered sail to be shortened and the fleet to jog off and on until daylight. At the break of day they made full sail, passed the southern point of the island, and sought an opening on the west coast through the barrier reef. Before noon they found it, sailed into a shallow bay, and anchored in the lee of the land, in five fathoms.

Here on a gleaming beach of white coral occurred the famous first landing of Columbus. The commander (now by general consent called Admiral) went ashore in the flagship's longboat displaying the royal standard of Castile, accompanied by the two Captains Pinzón in their boats, flying the banner of the expedition – a green crowned cross on a white field. "And, all having rendered thanks to our Lord, kneeling on the ground, embracing it with tears of joy for the immeasurable mercy of having reached it, the Admiral rose and gave this island the name *San Salvador*" - Holy Saviour.

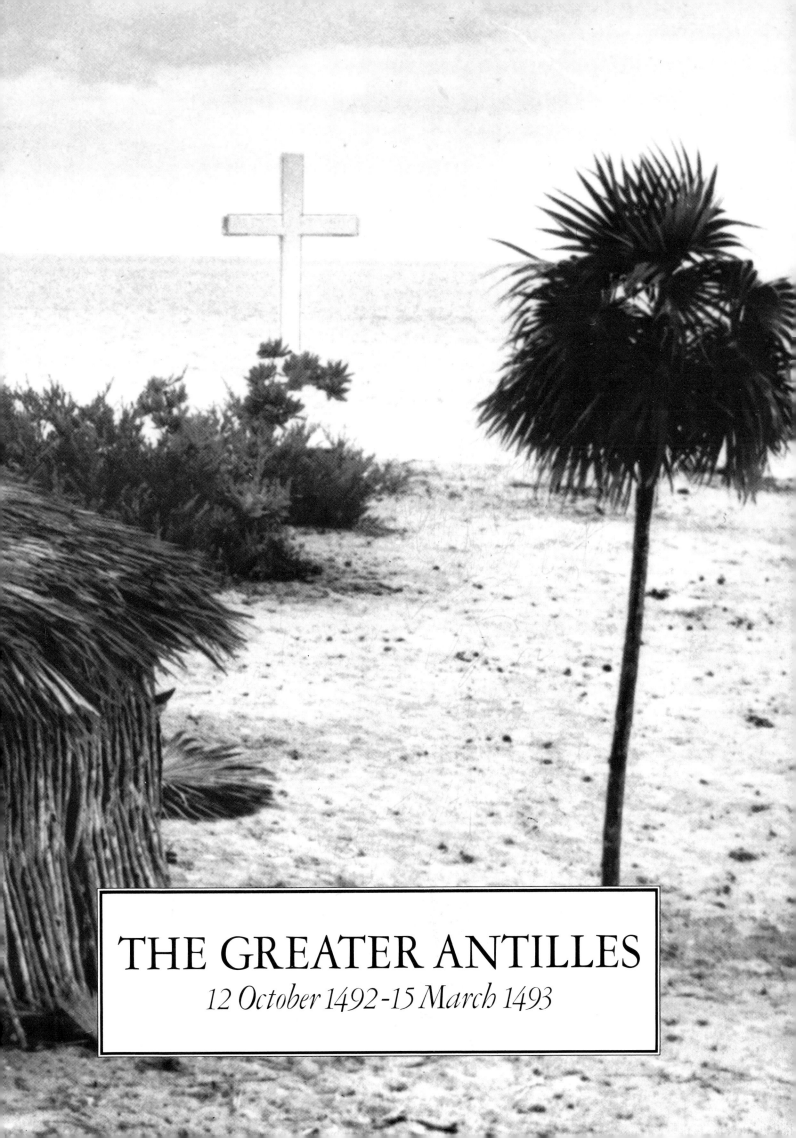

THE GREATER ANTILLES
12 October 1492–15 March 1493

South to Cuba

The first natives encountered on Guana-haní (their own name for this island) fled to the jungle when they saw three winged monsters approaching; but curiosity proved too much for them, and when they saw strangely dressed human beings coming ashore, they approached timidly, with propitiatory gifts. Columbus, of course, had to believe that he was in the Indies, so he named these people "Indians," and Indians the native inhabitants of the Americas have become in all European languages.

These were of the Taino branch of the Arawak language group. Within the previous century they had wrested the Bahamas and most of Cuba from the more primitive Siboney. They grew corn, yams, and other roots for food; they knew how to make cassava bread, to spin and weave cotton, and to make pottery. The Spaniards observed with wonder their fine physique and almost complete nakedness, and noted with interest that some wore, suspended from the nose, little pendants of pure gold. The guilelessness and generosity of these children of nature – "They invite you to share anything that they possess, and show

PAGES 64-65: Replicas of Arawak huts adorn the San Salvador beach where Columbus is said to have landed on 12 October, 1492.

RIGHT: Maybe the most familiar of Columbian icons is this scene of the Admiral's landing on San Salvador.

BELOW: A sketch in the Albertis collection in Genoa traces the route taken by Columbus on his First Voyage.

the Admiral knew full well that, interesting as the discovery of an island inhabited by Golden Age natives might be, he must take home certain evidence of Japan or China, or plenty of gold and spices, to prove his voyage a success. The natives indicated by sign language that scores of islands lay to the west and south; it seemed to the Admiral that these must be those shown on his chart, lying south of Cipangu; and that if they did not lead him to golden Japan, they would prove to be stepping-stones to China.

So, detaining six Indians as guides, Columbus weighed anchors on the after-

LEFT: The great cross marking the spot on a San Salvador beach where Columbus is said to have first set foot in the New World.

BELOW: A map of San Salvador showing the presumed route taken by Columbus's fleet.

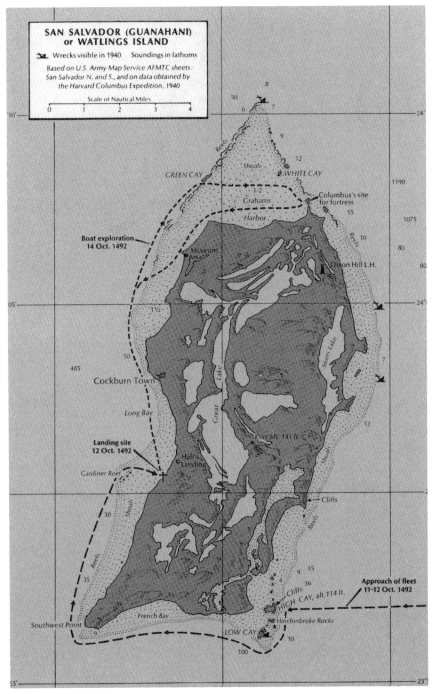

as much love as if their hearts went with it," wrote Columbus – their ignorance of money and of iron, and their nudity, suggested to every educated European that these people were holdovers from the Golden Age. Peter Martyr, the court historian, wrote that "They seem to live in that golden world of the which old writers speak so much, wherein men lived simply and innocently without enforcement of laws, without quarreling, judges and libels, content only to satisfy nature."

Columbus would much rather have encountered sophisticated Orientals than "noble savages," but as usual he made the best of the situation. He observed "how easy it would be to convert these people – and to make them work for us." In other words, to enslave them in return for saving their souls. Every Spaniard seems to have concluded from the tales of the mariners who returned from this voyage that no white man need do a hand's turn of work in the New World; God had provided docile natives to labor for the lords of creation.

For two days Columbus explored San Salvador. It was a pretty island then, with a heavy covering of tropical hardwood; but

Among Columbus's many botanical discoveries: *batatas hispaniorium*, or the sweet potato.

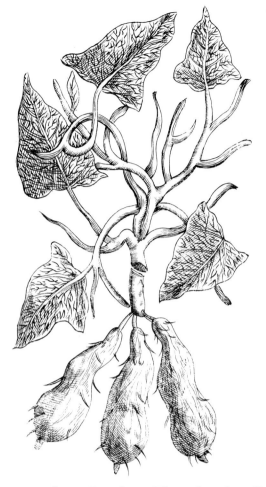

The natives here proved to be similar to those on San Salvador and were equally pleased with the Admiral's gifts of red caps, glass beads, and hawks' bells. These were little spherical bells about the diameter of a quarter-dollar or shilling, which were attached to the birds used in falconry; they had the pleasant tinkle of a miniature sleighbell, and the natives loved them. Indians would paddle out to the flagship wagging their fingers and saying, *Chuq! chuq!* meaning, "More hawks' bells, please!" Lace points, which were metal tips for the laces then used to fasten men's clothing, brass tambourine jingles, and Venetian glass beads were also favorites.

The Admiral's native guides, eager to please, kept assuring him by signs that in the next island there would plenty of gold; but each one in succession – Long, Crooked, and Fortune – proved to be no different from San Salvador. Each was jungle-covered, inhabited by friendly natives who had no gold except for a new ornaments which they had obtained elsewhere. Where they got them he could never make out, because of the language barrier; Torres, the interpreter, found his Arabic completely useless. The Spaniards observed, and Columbus noted, the first maize or Indian corn ever seen by a European, the first hammocks, woven from native cotton, and the first yams and sweet potatoes; also, a tree that he estimated correctly would prove to be good dye-wood. But no sign of gold except on the natives' persons.

As the Admiral and his Indian guides came to understand each other better, he heard about a big island that they called *Colba* (Cuba), and made up his mind that this must be either Japan or part of China. So to Colba he much go, and the Indians took him there by their usual canoe route, so laid out as to be the shortest possible jump over blue water.

First they sailed due west from Rum Cay to the northern end of Long Island, which they could see from the mastheads. *Fernandina*, as Columbus named Long Island, he described as very green, level, and fertile, and the natives friendly. He anchored off a village, and next day (17 October) investigated a *maravilloso puerto* – a marvelous harbor. Entering by a high bluff, he found it big enough to hold a hundred

Some gold from the New World recovered from the wreck of a Spanish galleon. Perhaps his failure to find major gold sources during any of his four voyages was Columbus's single greatest misfortune.

noon of 14 October. That day he discovered another island which he named *Santa Maria de la Concepción*; the English prosaically renamed it Rum Cay. This is still one of the prettiest Bahamian islands; hilly, well timbered, free of development blight. Today it has only about one hundred inhabitants clustered in a small village ambitiously called Port Nelson. The island has no roads, and a virgin forest covers it.

ships, "if it were deep, and clean bottom, and deep at the entrance," which unfortunately it was not. This description perfectly fits Santa Maria Harbor just east of the cape of that name. You enter it around high limestone cliffs, where there is now a small lighthouse, and it has water enough for small craft, but is much too shoal for a caravel or any other seagoing vessel.

While a shore party filled water casks from a well (one that is still used, since fresh water is scarce in the Bahamas), Columbus, in his own words, "walked among some trees, which were the most beautiful thing to see that ever I had seen, viewing as much verdure in so great a development as in the month of May in Andalusia, and all the trees were as different from ours as day from night, and so the fruits, the herbage, the rocks, and all things." This is a good example of his rapturous descriptions of scenery, flora, and natives, in which he stands out from all other discoverers and explorers of that era.

Sailing to the south end of Long Island on the 18th, Columbus decided to cross the Crooked Island Passage, now an important sea route to Cuba. Next day he ordered his ships to fan out on an easterly course so that they would not miss the next island – Crooked Island, which he named *Isabel* after the Queen. Here again he writes about the scenery ecstatically, and even notes the "fair and sweet smell of flowers or trees from the land . . . sweetest in the world." As we hove-to in the lee of this land in 1940, the land breeze similarly favored us with delicious odors.

Finding much to admire but nothing to detain him at Crooked and Fortune Islands, Columbus sailed back across Crooked Island Passage to the line of cays at the southwest edge of the Great Bahama Bank. On 27 October, from an anchorage off Ragged Island, the fleet made a fast sail with a fresh northeast wind to a big island which the Indians pointed out as "Colba." And on the morning of 28 October they entered a Cuban harbor easily identified as Bahia Bariay. It is marked by a beautiful mountain now called La Teta de Bariay, which Columbus said had "on its summit another peak like a pretty little mosque." He had never seen so beautiful a harbor – trees all fair and green and different from ours, some with bright flowers and some

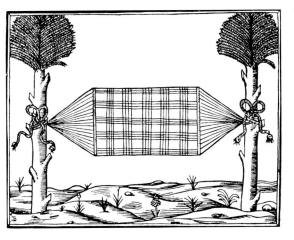

This drawing in a 1547 book is an artist's idea of an American Indian hammock, based on explorers' reports.

heavy with fruit, and the air full of birdsong. But where was the evidence of Japan? Where were the gold-roofed temples, dragon-mouthed bronze cannon? Where were the lords and ladies in gold-stiffened brocade?

Next day the three ships sailed westward along the many-harbored coast of Oriente Province of Cuba, hoping every moment to meet a welcoming fleet of Chinese junks. They anchored in Puerto Gibara, and there

An English artist's concept of Columbus's meeting with an Indian cacique in Cuba.

ABOVE: An Indian smoking: a detail from de Bry's 1590 *Grandes Voyages*.

ABOVE RIGHT: A view of Fernandina (Long Is.) in the Bahamas.

The tobacco plant, or *herba sancta* as it was dubbed by botanists in Europe, was certainly one of Columbus's more influential incidental discoveries.

remained for twelve days, except for a brief jaunt westward to Punta Cobarrubia and back.

The interpreters shipped at San Salvador assured local Indians that the strangers in the white-winged monsters were good people, with plenty of trading truck, so Columbus's Cuban relations were pleasant and peaceful. The natives told him that plenty of gold could be found at *Cubana-can* (mid-Cuba) in the interior. The Admiral, mistaking this word for *El Gran Can*, the Great Khan, sent an "embassy" up country to present his letter of introduction to the Chinese emperor; he remained in Puerto Gibara to oversee the beaching and graving of his ships. Luis de Torres the Arabic scholar took charge of this diplomatic mission, and beside him trudged Rodrigo de Jerez, a seaman who had once met a black king in Guinea and so was thought to know the proper way to address pagan royalty. They carried the diplomatic portfolio (Latin passport and royal letter of credence to the Grand Khan), strings of glass beads to buy food, and a gift suitable for royalty. The embassy tramped up the valley of the Cacoyuguin River, past fields cultivated with corn, beans, and sweet potatoes, to what they hoped would be Cambaluk, the imperial city of Cathay. Alas, it turned out to be a village of about fifty palm-thatched huts, on the site of the present town of Holguin. The two Spaniards, regarded as having come from above, were feasted by the local cacique while the populace swarmed up to kiss their feet and present simple gifts. Rodrigo the sailor loved it – he had never had it so good in Africa – but Torres, expecting a reception by mandarins in a stone-built capital of ten thousand houses, felt badly let down.

Yet on their way back to the harbor, the embassy made a discovery which would have more far-reaching results than any possible treaty. They met "many people who were going to their villages, both

women and men, with a firebrand in the hand and herbs to drink the smoke thereof, as they are accustomed." You have guessed it, reader; this was the first European contact with tobacco smokers. The Tainos used it in the form of cigars which they called *tobacos*. A walking party, such as the embassy encountered, would carry and large cigar and at every halt light it from a firebrand; everyone then took three or four "drags" of the smoke through his nostrils; after this refreshment the march resumed, small boys keeping the firebrand alight until the next stop. Not long after Spaniards settled in the New World, they tried smoking tobacco and liked it, and through them its use spread rapidly through Europe, Asia, and Africa.

Columbus, in the meantime, totted up his dead reckoning and figured that he was right where China began. He decided that Cuba was the "Province of Mangi," a name which the imaginative maps of China that he had seen located on a peninsula at the southest corner of the Celestial Empire. The Admiral also tried to shoot the North Star with his primitive quadrant. But he picked the wrong star – Alfirk of the constellation Cepheus – which on that November evening hung directly over Polaris. Thus he found Cuba to be on latitude 42° N, that of Cape Cod! Of course he knew this to be wrong, since he had sailed across on 28° N; and in his Letter to the Sovereigns he corrected the latitude of northern Cuba to 26°, still 5 degrees too high.

Here the Admiral began to collect specimens which he hoped would convince people that he was at least on the fringe of Asia. There was a shrub which smelled something like cinnamon and so must be

Having discovered the Greater Antilles on his First Voyage, the Admiral proceeded to discover the Lesser Antilles on his second. Here, a view of the coast of Basse Terre, Guadeloupe.

cinnamon; the gumbo-limbo, supposedly an Asiatic form of the gum mastic he had seen in Chios; and a small inedible nut, now called *nogal del pais*, he identified as the bog coconut mentioned by Marco Polo. Coconut palms are such a feature of the Caribbean coast today that we forget that they, like the banana, were introduced later. The men dug up some roots which Sánchez the surgeon pronounced to be Chinese rhubard, a valuable drug imported into Europe, but it turned out to be something quite different, not even as valuable as the humble pieplant.

As yet, no gold. When the Spaniards asked for gold, the Cubans always waved them on to some other place. According to

A Coco palm in India. The fact that Columbus found similar trees on the islands which he discovered can only have buttressed his conviction that he had in fact reached Asia.

them, there was an island called Babeque where the people gathered gold on the beach by candlelight and hammered it into bars. This choice piece of misinformation brought about the first rift in the Spanish high command. Without asking the Admiral's permission, Martín Alonso Pinzón took off in *Pinta*, hoping to be the first to reach Babeque. He called at Great Inagua Island, which lay in the general direction indicated by the Indians, and, needless to say, found no gold by candle or any other light.

The Admiral in *Santa Maria* with *Niña* sailed eastward along the superb coast of Oriente Province. Noble mountains rise directly from the sea, but every few miles there is a river whose mouth makes a good land-locked harbor. He called at Bahia Tánamo, entered its bottle-neck entrance, and within noted little wooded islands running up "like diamond points" and others flat-topped "like tables." You can see them all today. He put in at Puerto Cayo Moa, where you may have to pick an opening through the breakers but then find yourself, as Columbus said, in "a lagoon in which all the ships of Spain could lie and be safe." The peculiar charm of this harbor, so calm between lofty mountains and the barrier of foaming reefs, was noted by Columbus in words that are not in the least exaggerated. He had an eye, too, for practical matters; when the men rowed him inside the river mouth, he observed on the mountain slopes pine trees which he said would make timber for the Spanish navy. The descendants of those pines, when we passed that way, were being sawed at a mill run by a mountain stream, whose distant roar Columbus heard on a Sunday in November 1492.

On he sailed, with a breeze that fortunately came from the west, noting nine little harbors, behind which leafy valleys ran up into the lofty sierra. He passed the anvil-shaped mountain El Yunque, landmark for Baracoa, a harbor which Columbus well described as round "like a little porringer." Here the Spaniards pitched their first settlement in Cuba in 1512; but Baracoa afforded no gold, and the fleet passed on as soon as the wind turned fair. At sunrise 5 December it was off Cape Maisi, easternmost point of Cuba. Identifying this as the eastern extremity of Asia, corresponding to Cape St. Vincent, the western extremity of Europe, Columbus named it Cape Alpha and Omega, where East ends and West begins. He later remarked that if you had the time and strength, you could walk from here around the back of the world, to Spain!

Hispaniola

The fleet now crossed the Windward Passage, and at nightfall arrived off the Haitian harbor of San Nicolás, so named by Columbus because he entered it on 6 December, the feast day of that favorite saint of children. It is still St. Nicholas Mòle. His Indian guides promised that gold would be found on this great island, the home of their ancestors, and they were right. This island saved Columbus's reputation, for had he returned home with no more "evidence" than hitherto he had obtained, people would have said, "This Genoese has found a few islands inhabited by gentle natives of the Golden Age, but as for their being the Indies – pooh!"

And what beauty! I sailed the same waters in January 1939, deck passenger on a chaloupe of the Haitian Coast Guard. The shores were lined with bayahonde and other great tropical trees which Columbus mistook for clove and nutmeg. At night the Southern Cross was poised like a great kite over the headland that Columbus named *Cabo del Estrella* (Cape of the Star); and in the northern sky the Great Bear stood up on his tail.

A fair breeze took *Santa Maria* and *Niña* into Moustique Bay, where easterly winds detained them for five days. Here the Admiral, "seeing the grandeur and beauty of this island and its resemblance to the land of Spain," named it *La Isla Española* – the Spanish Isle. His seamen captured a young and beautiful girl wearing only a golden nose plug, and brought her on board. She indicated that she would gladly

Columbus's own sketch of the northwest part of "La Isla Española," later to be known as Hispaniola.

Illustrations from the 1493 book *Columbus's Letter to Sanchez*. On the left, an imaginary Spanish settlement on Hispaniola, and, right, an equally fanciful shallow-water galley cruising the waters off the island's coast.

Within five years of the discovery of the New World artists in Europe were rendering what would come to be known as "Americans" in this fashion.

well named the Valley of Paradise. Next day, when the fleet lay off a beach, some five hundred people came down accompanied by their youthful cacique, who made the Admiral a state visit. Bedecked with gold jewelry, he dined alone with the Admiral in his cabin and behaved with royal poise and dignity. Dinner over, Columbus had the cacique piped over the side in naval style and given a twenty-one-gun salute. Again the thought passed through his mind that these people were ripe for exploitation – "very cowardly," and "fit to be ordered about and made to work, to sow, and do aught else that may be needed." A wonderful opportunity, he observed, for his Sovereigns, whose subjects were not notably fond of hard work!

At sunrise 20 December the ships were off Acul Bay, the beauty of which was so striking that the Admiral ran out of adjectives describing it in his Journal; declared that all "ancient mariners" on board would bear him out. In 23 years at sea he had never seen so perfect a harbor as the one here, landlocked so completely that even in a blow one's anchor cable does not stretch taut. The high mountains part to reveal a conical peak at the head of the valley, which since 1806 has been crowned by the stone citadel of Henri Christophe, king of Haiti. Here the natives of 1492 were in an

stay with the boys, but the Admiral "sent her ashore very honorably," decently clad in slopchest clothing and bedecked with jingles and hawks' bells. This move proved to be good for public relations, as the damsel was a cacique's daughter. Next day nine Spaniards ashore were conducted to a big village of a thousand people and given everything they wanted – food, drink, girls, and parrots.

On 15 December *Santa Maria* and *Niña* beat up the Tortuga Channel to the mouth of Trois Rivières, a clear mountain stream that flows through a valley that Columbus

A map of the northern coast of Hispaniola, showing the site of Navidad and the place where *Santa Maria* was wrecked.

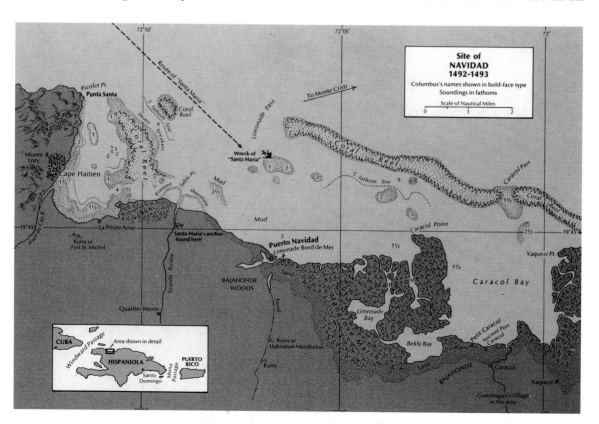

even more pristine state of innocence than elsewhere; the women, completely naked, had "very pretty bodies," and no male jealousy prevented their offering themselves freely. Moreover, these natives appeared to have plenty of gold.

During the night of 22-23 December and the following morning, about a thousand people came out in canoes to visit *Santa Maria*, and some five hundred more swam out, although she anchored more than three miles from the nearest shore. A messenger now arrived from Guacanagarí, the cacique of Marien (the northwestern part of Haiti), and a more important potentate than the one entertained a few days earlier. Guacanagarí sent the Admiral a magnificent belt with a solid-gold buckle, and invited him to call. He needed no second invitation, since everyone assured him that the gold mines were in that direction, the central part of the island called Cibao,

which suggested Cipangu, Japan. So, before sunrise on 24 December, *Santa Maria* and *Niña* departed Acul Bay, all hands planning to spend a merry Christmas at the court of the cacique, who might even turn out to be the emperor of Japan!

Fate decreed otherwise. With a contrary wind, the two vessels were unable to cover the few miles between Acul and Guacanagarí's capital on Caracol Bay by daylight. At 11:00 p.m., when the watch was changed, *Niña* and *Santa Maria* were becalmed east of Cape Haitien, inside the Limonade Pass to the barrier reef. Everyone on board was exhausted from the previous all-night entertainment of the natives; and as the water was calm, with only a slight ground swell and no wind, a feeling of complete security – the most dangerous delusion a seaman can entertain – stole over the flagship. Even the Admiral retired to get his first sleep in forty-eight

The Spanish government built the first modern replica of *Santa Maria* in 1892, and it was a subject of controversy almost from the start. Critics challenged its beam-to-length ratio, the design of its poopdeck and quarterdeck, the cut of its sails, even the dimensions of the vertical timbers along its sides. Certainly it proved to be some 25 percent slower than the original. But the fact remains that even today we still cannot be perfectly sure how this most famous of all ships really looked.

When, on his Fourth Voyage, Columbus saw a village of Indian huts such as these, built on stilts over water, he named the place by applying the Spanish diminutive for Venice: Venezuela.

hours; the helmsman gave the big tiller to a small boy and joined the rest of the watch in slumber.

Just as midnight ushered in Christmas Day, *Santa Maria* settled on a coral reef so gently that nobody awoke with the shock. The boy helmsman, feeling the rudder ground, sang out; the Admiral came first on deck, followed by Master Juan de La Cosa and all hands. As the bow had only grounded, Columbus saw a good chance to get her off stern first, and ordered La Cosa and a boat's crew to run an anchor out astern. Instead of obeying orders, they rowed to *Niña*, which had passed well outside the reef. Captain Pinzón refused to receive them, and sent a boat of his own ship.

But an hour had been wasted, owing to La Cosa's cowardice or insubordination, and that doomed *Santa Maria*. The ground swell drove her higher and higher up the reef, and coral heads punched holes in her bottom. As the hull seemed to be filling with water, Columbus ordered abandon ship, hoping that daylight would make it easier to float her. Guacanagarí and his subjects worked hard with the Spaniards to get her off after daybreak, but it was too late. All they could salvage were the equipment, stores, and trading truck, which the Indians faithfully guarded without (so the Admiral recorded) purloining so much as a lace point.

The Admiral tried to figure out what this apparently disastrous accident meant. Presently he had it: God intended him to start a colony at that point, with *Santa Maria*'s crew. Guacanagarí begged him to do so, as he wanted help against enemies elsewhere on the island. The Spaniards fell over each other to volunteer, because signs of gold were now so plentiful that they were confident of making their fortunes. So Columbus gave orders to erect a fortified camp ashore and named it *Villa de la Navidad* (Town of the Nativity) in honor of the day of disaster, which he fondly thought God had turned to his advantage.

Navidad, first attempt by Europeans since the Northmen to establish themselves in the New World, was quickly built, largely out of *Santa Maria*'s timbers. It was probably located on the sandspit now called Limonade Bord-de-Mer, off which there is good anchorage. Sixteen men from the flagship and five from *Niña* volunteered to stay behind, under the command of Columbus's Cordovan friend Diego de Harana. The Admiral gave them a share of his provisions, most of the trading truck, and the flagship's boat. They were instructed to explore the country with a view to finding a permanent settlement, to trade for gold, and to treat the natives kindly.

Columbus was now certain that he had found the Indies.

On the day after New Year's 1493, Guacanagarí and Columbus held a farewell party. *Niña* fired cannon balls through what was left of the hull of *Santa Maria* to impress the natives, and the cacique feasted all hands. After final expressions of mutual love and esteem, the allies parted and the Admiral went on board *Niña*, to return home in her. At sunrise 4 January she set sail, and the homeward passage began.

Homeward Passage

Two days later, Columbus sighted *Pinta* sailing in a contrary direction, down-wind. Martín Alonso came on board and gave a fairly convincing account of his doings during the last three weeks. He had called at the Great Inagua, ascertained that the yarn about picking up gold by candlelight was a myth, then sailed along the coast of Hispaniola and anchored in Puerto Blanco. There a shore party penetrated the Cibao and found plenty of gold. Pinzón had heard of the flagship's wreck by Indian "grapevine," and so sailed back to lend the Admiral a hand. Columbus, pleased to have company on the voyage home, decided to let bygones be bygones.

While waiting for a fair wind to double

ABOVE: Columbus's son Diego in 1510 erected this castle in Santo Domingo, Hispaniola.

BELOW: Still another Columbian botanical find was this variety of pineapple.

Surf on Puerto Rico. During his exploration of northern Hispaniola on the First Voyage Columbus came close to discovering this great neighboring island. He would do so within the year (1493) during his Second Voyage.

Monte Cristi peninsula, with its tent-like promontory behind which he anchored, Columbus explored by boat the lower course of the Rio Yaque del Norte and found gold nuggets as large as lentils. Even today there is gold in that river valley; the country women pan it out laboriously, and when they have enough to fill a turkey quill, they use it to pay for their shopping.

At midnight 8 January, *Niña* and *Pinta* resumed their homeward passage. Passing along the coast of Hispaniola, they looked in at *Puerto Plata* (so named by Columbus on account of silver clouds over the mountains) and anchored near the mouth of Samaná Bay. There, at a place still called *Punta de las Flechas*, the Spaniards encountered the first natives who were not pleased to meet them, and who were armed with bows and arrows. These were a branch of the Tainos called Ciguayos, who in self-defense against raiding Caribs had adopted their weapons. By dint of catching one Ciguayo, treating him well and sending him ashore with an assortment of red cloth and trinkets, the rest were appeased, and a brisk if somewhat cautious trade was conducted. Also, one or two were persuaded to join the native contingent bound for Spain.

On Wednesday, 18 January, three hours before daybreak, the caravels sailed from Samaná Bay. A rough, tough voyage lay ahead. This homeward passage was a far greater test of Columbus's seamanship and ability to handle men than anything he had hitherto undertaken. With the greatest geographical discovery of all time locked in his breast, knowing that it would be of no use to anybody unless delivered, the Admiral had to fight the elements and human weakness for his survival.

The west wind with which they took off

A Puerto Rican rain forest. In years to come, timber from Cuba and Puerto Rico would be of vital importance to the Spanish navy.

An old engraving of various seaweeds, many of which Columbus and his men must have seen when the fleet passed through the Sargasso Sea in January 1493.

soon petered out, easterly trade winds returned, and the caravels sailed as best they could, close-hauled on the starboard tack. Modern sailing craft can sail as close to the wind as four points (45 degrees) or, if very smart racers in smooth water, even closer. *Niña* and *Pinta* would lay up to five points (56 degrees) if the sea was smooth, but under ordinary conditions could not do better than 6 points (67½ degrees); and *Pinta* was slow on the wind, owing to a sprung mizzenmast. This meant, in practice, that if it blew from the southeast, the caravels could steer ENE; with a due east wind the best course toward Spain of which they were capable was NNE; and if it backed to NE (as the trade wind often does), the Admiral had to bring them about on the port tack and steer ESE.

In this manner *Niña* and *Pinta* continued through January of 1493, reaching further north and edging a little closer to Spain. As they were near the northern limit of the trades, the sea was smooth, and providentially the wind held and blew them across the horse latitudes, as seamen used to call the calms between latitudes 30° and 33° N. They crossed the Sargasso Sea, having the rare and beautiful experience of sailing with a fresh wind across an undulating meadow of gulfweed, under a full moon.

Boatswain birds, boobies, and the fork-tailed frigate bird were flying about; and one day the sea abounded in tunnies, which the Admiral (making the only humorous remark recorded in his writings) said he expected to end in the Duke of Cadiz's tunny factory at Cadiz. That name caused the seamen to lick their lips in anticipation of seeing again the Cadiz girls, famous through Europe for their saucy beauty and salty wit.

During this uneventful part of the voyage the Admiral took time and pains to write a report on his impressions to Ferdinand and Isabella. Of the natives he writes, "In their islands I have so far found no human monstrosities" (as everyone expected from John de Mandeville). "On the contrary . . . good looks are esteemed; nor are they blacks, as in Guinea, but with flowing hair." A glowing account of their products follows – gum mastic as in Chios, spices, cotton, aloes, slaves.

All go naked, men and women, as their mothers bore them, except that some women cover one place only with the leaf of a plant or with a net of cotton which they make for that. Although they are well-built people of handsome stature, they are wonderfully timorous. They have no other arms than arms of canes, and they dare not make

Columbus's discovery unleashed a wave of exploration unlike any in history, before or since. Two centuries later explorers such as Canada's Fr. Louis Hennepin had still not unraveled all the many mysteries of the vast new continent Columbus had found.

A New Difcovery of a Large Country in AMERICA by Father Lewis Hennepin

Columbus's ships on their return voyage in 1493, as imagined by *Harper's Monthly*. The artist has rigged the caravels fore-and-aft, even though Columbus explicitly says they were square-rigged.

kind may be given to them. I forbade that they should be given things so worthless as pieces of broken crockery and broken glass, and end of straps, although when they were able to get them, they thought they had the best jewel in the world; thus it was ascertained that a sailor for a strap received gold to the weight of two and half *castellanos*,[*] and others much more for other things which were worth much less; yea, for new *blancas*,[**] for them they would give all they had, although it might be two or three castellanos' weight of gold or an *arrova*[***] or two of spun cotton. . . . They believe very firmly that I, with these ships and people, came from the sky . . . and this does not result from their being ignorant, for they are of a very keen intelligence and men who navigate all those seas.

He particularly admired their dugout *canoas* (here that word enters European language) "made of a single log," carrying up to seventy or eighty men. His description of the scenery and the flora are ecstatic, and not exaggerated, except that he identified very ordinary and useless plants as spices or rare drugs.

Without knowing it, Columbus had followed the best sailing directions for reaching home quickly. Had he tried to sail straight across to Spain (as he did in 1496), he would have had to beat to windward most of the way; but this long northerly leg took him up to the latitude of Bermuda into the zone of rough, strong westerlies.

On the last day of January the wind swung into the west, and four days later, when the Admiral figured by a simple "eye sight" of the North Star that he had reached the latitude of Cape St. Vincent (and actually was on that of Gibraltar), he set the course due east, 90 degrees. Owing to compass variation, this worked out as about 80 degrees true, right for picking up the Azores. The weather now turned cold and a fresh gale made up. During four days the caravel made an average run of 150 miles, and at times attained a speed of 11 knots.

When any sailing yacht the length of *Niña* and *Pinta* hits it up to 11 or 12 knots today, you have something to talk about; and these caravels were having the finest

use of these. . . . After they have been reassured and have lost this fear, they are artless and so free with all they possess, that no one would believe it without having seen it. Of anything they have, if you ask them for it, they never say no; rather they invite the person to share it, and show as much love as if they were giving their hearts; they are content with whatever little thing of whatever

---

[*] $7.50 in gold.
[**] A copper coin worth half a maravedi, a fraction of a cent.
[***] A weight equivalent to 25 lbs, or 11½ kilos.

kind of sailing. They were running before a fresh gale over deep blue, white-crested water. On they sped through bright, sunny days and nights brilliant with Orion and other familiar constellations that seemed to be beckoning them home. It is hard for any sailor to be sorry for Columbus, in spite of his later misfortunes; he enjoyed such glorious sailing weather on almost every voyage. But he had some very tough experiences, and one of the worst was about to come.

The westerly gale died down by nightfall 7 February, and for two days the caravels had light variables and made little progress. On the ninth they were able to square again eastward. Next day the pilots and captains held a ship-to-ship discussion of their position. Everyone, including Columbus, thought they were much further south than they actually were, and all except the Admiral put them on the meridian of the eastern Azores; but Columbus estimated correctly that they were almost due south of Flores, and decided to call at one of the Azores, if possible.

He very nearly didn't make it. The two caravels were sailing into an area of dirty water in one of the coldest and most blustery winters on record – a winter in which hundreds of vessels went down, scores crashed ashore, ships lay windbound at Lisbon for months, and the harbor of Genoa froze over. The center of the an area of very low pressure was passing north of the Azores with southwest to west winds

The Age of Discovery begun by Columbus and the Portuguese spurred the art of celestial navigation, and soon elaborate planispheres such as this became commonplace features in marine atlases.

RIGHT: A lagoon on the Venezuelan coast. It was only on his Third Voyage that Columbus realized that he had at last discovered the mainland he sought.

BELOW: An engraving of the dramatic scene in the return voyage when Columbus, afraid his ship will founder in a storm, has a cask containing a summary of his journal thrown into the sea.

of full gale strength, and the caravels had to pass through three weather fronts.

Niña, stripped down to bare poles, on 12 February scudded before the wind, laboring heavily. The wind moderated slightly next morning, then increased, and the little caravel ran into frightful seas. The elongated isobaric system brought opposite winds very close to one another, and the resulting cross seas formed dangerous pyramidical waves that broke over the caravels from stern to stern. With only her reefed main course set, and the yard slung low, *Niña* sailed in a general northeasterly direction, while the Admiral and Captain Pinzón took turns as officer of the deck, watching every wave to warn the helmsman below. One mistake by either, and she would have broached-to, rolled over and sunk, and *Pinta* could never have rescued survivors in such a sea.

The following night, 13-14 February, the two caravels lost sight of each other and never met again that side of Spain. We have no record of how *Pinta* fared, but *Niña*'s crew almost gave up hope on St. Valentine's Day. Thrice, officers and men drew lots for one to go on a pilgrimage to some famous shrine if they were saved; but the wind only blew harder. Then they all made a vow "to go in procession in their shirts" to the first shrine of the Virgin they might encounter. The wind then began to abate. Columbus afterward admitted that he was as frightened as anyone. Desperate lest both ships and all hands perish, at the height of the gale he wrote on a parchment an abstract of his journal of the voyage, wrapped it in waxed cloth, headed it up in a cask, and hove it overboard in the hope that someone might pick up the true story of his discovery. The cask was never recovered but sundry faked-up versions of the Admiral's "Secrete Log Boke" are still being offered to credulous collectors.

Shortly after sunrise 15 February, land was sighted dead ahead. Columbus correctly guessed that it was one of the Azores, he dared not guess which. The wind then whipped into the east, and three days elapsed before *Niña* was able to come up to this island and anchor. The Admiral sent his boat ashore and ascertained that it was Santa Maria, southernmost of the group. He anchored near a village called Nossa Senhora dos Anjos (Our Lady of the Angels), where a little church was dedicated to the Virgin, who had appeared surrounded by angels to a local fisherman. Anjos was an answer to prayer, and the proper place for the crew to fulfill their vow made at the height of the storm.

There then took place what, in retrospect, seems really comic. Here were men bursting with the greatest piece of news in centuries, a discovery that would confer untold benefits on all Europeans; yet, how were they, and it, received? While saying their prayers in the chapel, clad only in their shirts (as a sign of penitence), half the crew was set upon by "the whole town" and thrown into jail. The Portuguese captain of the island suspected that they had been on an illicit voyage to West Africa! He even rowed out, hoping to capture Columbus and a few members of *Niña*'s crew who had stayed on board, intending to make their pilgrimage later. The Admiral refused to receive him and threatened to shoot up the town and carry off hostages if his people were not released. Before the captain could make up his mind, another storm blew up. *Niña*'s cables parted, and she was blown almost to São Miguel and back. And she did well to get back, because only three seamen and the Indians were left on board to help the Admiral and the skip-

per. By the time *Niña* returned, the Portuguese captain, having grilled the captured sailors and discovered no evidence of poaching on royal preserves, surrendered them and furnished the entire crew with much-need fresh provisions.

Columbus resumed his homeward voyage on 24 February 1493. The distance to his desired landfall, Cape St. Vincent, was only 800 miles, which should have required only a week's sail in the prevailing north wind. But this piece of ocean in winter is a place where low-pressure areas hang around and make trouble for sailors, and the winter of 1493 was unusually foul. Another tempest overtook *Niña* about 250 miles from Santa Maria and stayed with her all the way, giving her an even worse beating than did the storm west of the Azores.

Two days out from Santa Maria, trouble began. The wind shifted to southeast, forcing *Niña* to change course to ENE. Next day both wind and sea made up, and for three days they were blown off their course. On the night of 2 March the warm front of the circular storm hit *Niña*, the wind changed to southwest, and she was able to sail her course; but that same night the cold front overtook her with a violent

ABOVE: A quadrant of 1520. It was not very useful to sailors, but its descendant, the sextant would prove to be indispensible.

BELOW: By an ancient tradition of the sea, marine compass cards were divided into 32 points corresponding to the points of sail.

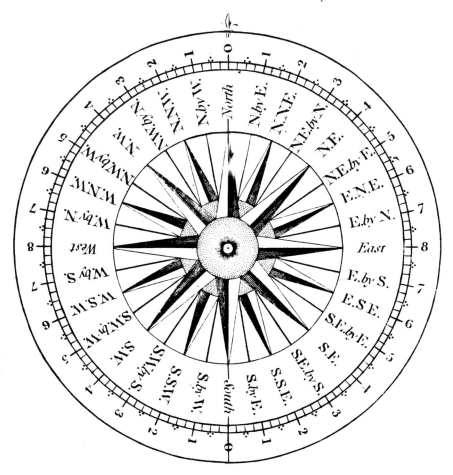

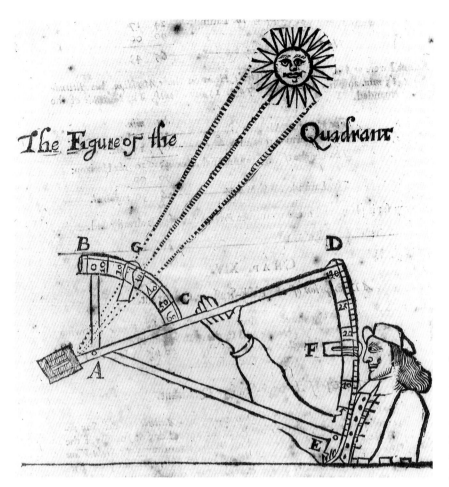

The Figure of the Quadrant

B G C D F A E

An elaborate quadrant of the late sixteenth century. It's eye-piece and reflecting mirror are ancestral features of the sextants and octants of later times.

A seventeenth-century engraving that shows Columbus looking rather like a jovial pirate captain.

squall which split the main course and blew the furled foresail and mizzen out of their gaskets, whipping them to ragged ribbons. Columbus did the only thing he could do, forge ahead under bare poles. *Niña* pitched and rolled frightfully in cross seas and the wind made another shift, to northwest, on 3 March. This was the backlash of the cyclone, worse than the forelash. As the dark winter afternoon waned, anxiety became intense. Columbus and the pilots knew by dead reckoning that they were driving right on to the ironbound coast of Portugal, and that only a miracle could prevent a fatal crash against the cliffs.

Shortly after six o'clock, when the sun set, the crisis came. Lightning flashed overhead, and great seas broke aboard from both sides. The wind blew so strong it "seemed to raise the caravel into the air." Fortunately, it was the night of full moon, which sent enough light through the clouds so that at seven o'clock land was sighted dead ahead, distant perhaps fives miles. Columbus then performed the difficult maneuver, well known to every old-time seaman, of "clawing off" a lee shore. The coast ran north and south, the wind blew

from the northwest, so they set one little square foresail that had been saved intact, wore ship in a smother of foam, and shaped a course south, parallel to the coast, with wind on the starboard quarter. No wonder *Niña* became the Admiral's favorite vessel, to stand all that beating and respond to this difficult maneuver without broaching.

When day broke on 4 March, Columbus recognized prominent Cabo da Roca that juts into the ocean from the mountains of Sintra, just north of the entrance of the Tagus. With only one square sail between him and utter destruction, the Admiral naturally elected to enter the Tagus and call at Lisbon to refit, rather than to attempt to continue around Cape St. Vincent to Spain. He well knew that he was taking a great risk in placing himself in the power of D. João II, the monarch who had turned him down twice; but his first consideration was to get word of his discovery to Spain. So, after sunrise, *Niña* whipped around Cabo da Roca, passed Cascais where the fishermen were amazed to see so tiny a vessel coming in from the sea, crossed the smoking bar at the river mouth, and by nine

CHRISTOFEL COLONUS.

o'clock anchored off Belém, the outerport of Lisbon.

To be safely anchored in a snug harbor after long tossing at sea gave the sailors a wonderful feeling of relief, but the Admiral and his battered crew still had plenty to worry about. *Niña* would have to be refitted before proceeding to Spain, and would the Portuguese allow it? And what had happened to *Pinta*?

The first Portuguese gesture was not assuring. Moored near *Niña* was a large warship, the name of whose master was Bartholomew Dias – not, apparently, the discoverer of the Cape of Good Hope. Dias came over in an armed boat and ordered Columbus to report on board and give an account of himself. The Admiral stood on his dignity and refused; but he showed his credentials, which satisfied both Dias and his captain. Columbus had already sent a letter to D. João asking permission to enter Lisbon, and on 8 March a nobleman brought the answer, which not only granted his request – ordering that *Niña* be supplied with all she needed – but invited the Admiral to visit the king at his country residence. Columbus decided he

had better accept, although he feared lest visiting the King of Portugal before reporting to the Queen of Castile would offend her – as indeed it did. So, selecting two or three followers and some of the healthiest of his captive Indians, Columbus landed at Lisbon and chartered a train of mules to take himself and his suite up-country. Pity the poor Indians who, after their terrible buffeting at sea, must now suffer the rigors of muleback transport along the narrow, muddy roads of Portugal! It took them two days to make the thirty-mile journey to the monastery of Santa Maria das Virudes, where the King was then staying.

D. João received Columbus with unexpected graciousness, but his court chronicler tells us that he was really furious with the Admiral and suspected that the new discoveries had been made in a region where Portugal had prior rights. Courtiers urged the King to have this boastful upstart discreetly assassinated, as he had recently disposed of an annoying brother-in-law. Fortunately, he refused. And the King had to admit that his Indian guests looked very different from any Africans he had ever

Early merchant ships such as *Santa Maria*, with broad beams and built-up forecastles and sterns, were named *naos* or carracks. By the sixteenth century the *nao*'s features would be exaggerated to produce such large and imposing vessels as that pictured here.

seen or heard of. Two of them made a rough chart of the Antilles with beans, convincing the King, who smote his breast and cried out, "Why did I let slip such a wonderful chance?"

On 11 March Columbus and his suite departed, escorted by a troop of cavaliers, and made a detour to call on the Queen of Portugal at the Convent of Santo António da Castanheira. The Admiral was so sore from his muleback cruise that on reaching the Tagus he chartered a boat to take him down-river to *Niña*. During his absence she had been fitted with a new suit of sails and running rigging, and had taken on fresh provisions, wood, water, and wine.

She was now ready for the last leg of the voyage, all her crew were on board, and on the following morning, 13 March, the gallant little caravel weighed anchor from Lisbon.

Strange to relate, *Pinta* was following her, not far astern. She had missed the Azores, thus escaping the worst of the tempests that swept over *Niña*, and about the end of February, made Bayona near Vigo in northwest Spain. Here Martín Alonso Pinzón attempted to beat Columbus home with the great news. He sent a message across Spain to Ferdinand and Isabella at Barcelona, announcing his arrival and begging permission to come himself and tell

The malarial jungles surrounding the two trading posts which Columbus tried to set up on Hispaniola did as much to guarantee their failure as did any Indian hostility.

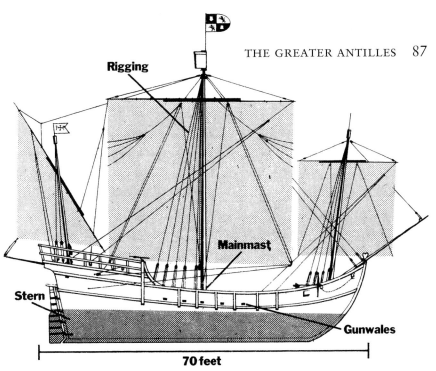

them about the voyage. The Sovereigns sent back word that they preferred to hear the news from Columbus himself. *Pinta* then sailed from Bayona for Palos.

Niña wore ship around Cape St. Vincent at daybreak 14 March and passed the beach where Columbus had swum ashore after the sea fight seventeen years earlier. At midday 15 March she crossed the bar of the Saltés and dropped anchor off Palos. *Pinta* followed on the same tide. The sight of *Niña* already there, snugged down as if she had been at home a month, finished Martín Alonso Pinzón. Older than Columbus, ill from the hardships of the voyage, mortified by his snub from the Sovereigns, he could bear no more. He went directly to his country house near Palos, took to his bed, and died within the month.

So ended, 224 days after it began, the greatest recorded voyage in history. Here is Columbus's final prophecy in his Letter to the Sovereigns:

> So, since our Redeemer has given this victory to our most illustrious King and Queen, and to their famous realms, in so great a matter, for this all Christendom ought to feel joyful and make celebrations and give solemn thanks to the Holy Trinity with many solemn prayers for the great exaltation which it will have, in the turning of so many peoples to our holy faith, and afterwards for material benefits, since not only Spain but all Christians will hence have refreshment and profit.

Most of what we think we know about caravels today is summed up in this 1985 sketch from the *New York Times*. In this case the caravel is square-rigged, but with a shift of masts it could be all lateen-rigged.

Florida Indians, as rendered by the French engraver Le Moyne de Morgues in the mid sixteenth-century.

TRIUMPH
March–June 1493

PAGES 88-89: Columbus returns to Spain.

BELOW: Holy Week in Seville.

BOTTOM: The Plaza di España in Seville.

Columbus had already sent a copy of his official report on the voyage from Lisbon to Barcelona. Fearing lest it miscarry or be impounded by D. João II, he now sent another copy to the Sovereigns by official courier, and a third to the municipality at Cordova. Before proceeding to Seville to await the reply, he fulfilled his vows at the local church and spent two weeks with Fray Juan Pérez and other friends at La Rábida. On Palm Sunday, 31 March, he entered Seville in time to take part in the traditional ceremonies of Holy Week.

Holy Week in Seville, with its alternation of humility and pride, penance and pardon, death and victory, seemed at once a symbol and a fitting conclusion to this great adventure. The daily processions of the brotherhoods with their gorgeously bedecked statues of saints, the ancient ceremonies in the Cathedral – rending of the temple veil, knocking at the great door, candles on the great *tenebrario* extinguished until but one remained, the washing of feet on Maundy Thursday, the supreme Passion on Good Friday when one heard the clacking of the *matraca* in place of cheerful bells, the consecration of the paschal candle, and the supreme ecstasy of Easter morn – all that moved Columbus as no worldly honors could, and strengthened his conviction that his own toils and triumphs fitted the framework of the Passion. And it was pleasant to receive the congratulations of old friends who "always knew he would make it," to be presented to noblemen and bishops, and to have young

caballeros introduced by their fathers in order to plead with Señor Almirante to take them to the Indies, where they would do anything he asked. (They meant, anything but work!)

What the Indian captives thought of it all we know not.

On or shortly after Easter Sunday, 7 April, the Admiral's cup of happiness overflowed upon receipt of a letter from Ferdinand and Isabella to "Don Cristóbal Colón, their Admiral of the Ocean Sea, Viceroy and Governor of the Islands that he hath discovered in the Indies." These were the exact titles they had promised him if he did reach the Indies, and the use of them indicated that they believed he had. They expressed pleasure at his achievements, commanded him to attend court, and "Inasmuch as we will that that which you have commenced with the aid of God be continued and furthered," ordered preparations for a second voyage to be started immediately.

Sweet words! Columbus promptly drafted a report for the Sovereigns on how Hispaniola should be colonized. As chance

The arms granted to Columbus. In the upper quarters, the castle of Castile and lion of León; in the lower, islands and anchors.

entries in his Journal prove, he had been thinking this over for several months. The result was a modification of the trading-factory idea with which he had begun his First Voyage. He now proposed to recruit two thousand settlers who would be required to build houses in a designated town in return for a license to trade for gold with the natives. Each must return to the town at stated intervals and hand over his gold for

The interior of the Alcazar, after the cathedral Seville's loveliest building.

RIGHT: Columbus makes his triumphal entry into Barcelona, where he will be received by the Spanish Sovereigns.

BELOW: An extravagant version of Columbus's meeting with Ferdinand and Isabella.

smelting to an official who would deduct the Sovereigns' fifth, the Admiral's tenth, and another tax to support the church. There should be a closed season on gold-hunting in order to ensure that the settlers would take time to grow crops. Foreigners, Jews, infidels, and heretics must be kept out of the Indies, but priests should be sent there to convert the natives.

Columbus had already realized from his contact with the Tainos that their wants were few and easily met, so that they could not be expected to flock to the beach to sell gold, as did the natives of Africa. To do much business, Spaniards would have to work the interior of Hispaniola and perhaps other islands too. But, in the interest of fiscal control, everyone must check in at a trading factory on the coast, and all transatlantic traffic must go through Cadiz.

After sending this report ahead by courier, the Admiral purchased clothes suitable for his rank, and organized a cavalcade, including a few of his officers and servants, and six long-suffering Indians in native dress to carry parrots in cages. At Cordova the municipality gave him a reception, and he met his mistress Beatriz and picked up his two sons to join him. They arrived at Barcelona around 20 April 1493. As he entered the hall of the Alcazar where the Sovereigns held court, his dignity, gray hair, and noble countenance tanned by eight months at sea made the learned men present compare him to a Roman senator. As he advanced to the throne to make obeisance, Ferdinand and Isabella arose; and when he knelt to kiss hands, they bade him rise, and seated him on the Queen's right. The Indians were presented, the gold artifacts and samples of alleged rare spices were examined, a multitude of questions asked and answered; then all adjourned to the chapel where *Te Deum* was chanted. It was observed that at the last line, "O Lord, in Thee have I trusted, let me never be confounded," tears were streaming down the Admiral's face.

Columbus at this point could have had anything he wanted – castle in Spain, title, pension, or endowment. It would have been well for him had he then taken his profits and retired with honor, leaving to others the responsibility of colonization. But he was not that kind of a man. Had he been, this great voyage would never have taken place. He must see that the islands he discovered were settled by Christians; he must put the gold trade on a proper footing, and start conversion of the natives; he must meet the Grand Khan or some Oriental potentate of higher rank than Guacanagarí. The rights already granted to him, incident to his offices of Admiral and Viceroy, promised to be far more lucrative than any estate in Spain; and so they would have been, had the crown respected them. Moreover, he was in good health, full of energy, in the prime of life (aged forty-one), and he regarded the work for which God had appointed him to be just begun.

His sense of a divine mission also appears in the curious Graeco-Latin signature he now adopted, and of which no contemporary explanation exists. In the entail of his property he describes it as "an X [by which he probably meant a Greek chi] with an S over it and an M with a Roman A over it and over that an S and then a Greek Y [by which he probably meant a capital upsilon] with an S over it, preserving the relation of the lines and points." The way he wrote it is as follows:

.S.
S.A.S
X.M.Y
:Xpo FERENS

Many attempts have been made to solve the riddle. My suggestion is that the initials

Barcelona's waterfront boulevard, the Passo de Colon, commemorates the Admiral's famous visit in 1493.

stand for *Servus Sum Altissimi Salvatoris, Christoû Mariae Yioû* (Servant am I of the Most High Savious, Christ Son of Mary). The last line, *Xpo Ferens,** is a Graeco-Latin form of *Christopher*, emphasizing his most cherished mission, to carry Christianity to lands beyond the sea. Even on such brief chits as have survived, he signed himself X*po* FERENS, the Christ Bearer.**

Columbus tarried at court over Whitsuntide, Trinity Sunday, and Corpus Christi. The King and Queen and Infante Don Juan having graciously consented to act as godparents, six Indians were baptized. The first in rank, kinsman to Guacanagarí, they christened "Ferdinand of Aragon"; another, "Don Juan of Castile";

*This is not to be read "Expo" but "christo," the letters Chi Rho being a common Greek abbreviation of *Christ*.
**Sometimes he signed himself "El Virrey"; and on one occasion, "Virrey de Asia."

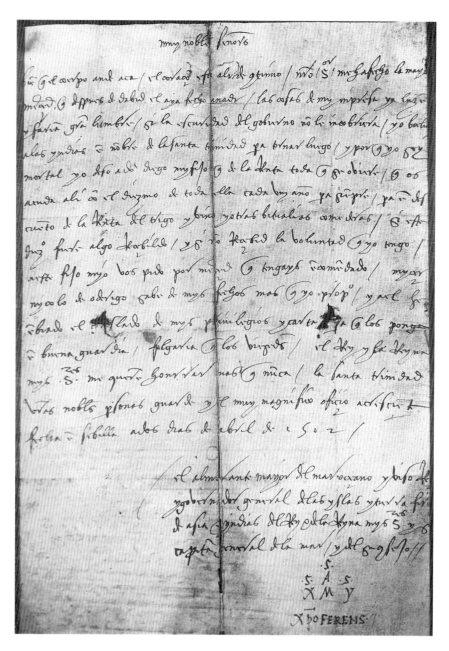

A page from a letter by Columbus showing, above the signature, the cryptic cypher he so often used. To this day its meaning is an unresolved mystery.

while the clever interpreter was named "Don Diego." Don Juan attached himself to the royal household and died within two years; the other five returned with the Admiral to the New World.

These christenings expressed good intentions of the Sovereigns and of Columbus toward the natives, but in the Indies themselves, human greed had to be satisfied first, and forced labor exterminated almost the entire native population of Hispaniola within half a century. But the Indians unwittingly had their revenge on Europeans through *Treponema pallida,* the spirochete of syphilis, which the conquerors contracted in the Indies and brought back to Spain. The first recorded outbreak of syphilis in Europe took place in 1494 among the soldiers of a French army which

marched to Naples and back. Bishop Las Casas, who admired Columbus, loved the Indians, and spent a large part of his life in a vain effort to protect them, states in his *Apologetica Historia* of around 1530 that the disease was transmitted to the French army by Spanish women who were infected by the Indians brought to Barcelona by Columbus. He adds that, from repeated questioning of the natives of Hispaniola, he believed the disease to be one of long standing in the New World; so long, indeed, that the natives did not suffer greatly from it. Among Europeans, however, syphilis promptly assumed the most hideous and malignant forms, with many fatalities, just as measles and smallpox affected the Indians when introduced by Europeans. It seems, therefore, probable that the Indians who Columbus brought to Barcelona were so joyfully and briskly entertained by the women of the town as to infect these women, who either infected Spanish volunteers in the army of Charles VIII or accompanied that army as camp followers.

This subject is controversial; but it appears to me that Las Casas was correct. *Niña*'s crew for the return voyage cannot have contracted syphilis, for all were healthy and able to work the ship up to the moment of landing; Columbus more than once remarked on it with amazement, since on African voyages sailors were expected to sicken and die. Medical authorities assure me that it would have been almost impossible for a man infected with syphilis to make a tough voyage of two months without becoming very sick indeed. As for those in *Pinta*, a Spanish surgeon named Ruy Día de Isla, in his book on the disease printed at Seville in 1539, stated that the spirochete infected "a pilot of Palos called Pinzón," and implies that he attended him. It will be remembered that three Pinzóns shipped in *Pinta*, and that Martín Alonso, the captain, died shortly after her arrival; but Díaz de Isla admits that the disease also spread from Barcelona. It became a terrible plague in Europe and among the Spanish colonists of Hispaniola. They used a local Indian remedy, decoctions of guiacum or lignum vitae. This had no therapeutic effect whatsoever, but people, both natives and Europeans, thought it to be a sovereign cure.

Although Columbus tarried several

weeks in Barcelona, he did not simply bask in the sunshine of royalty. He looked after their interests, and his own. The Sovereigns' letters patent granting him a coat of arms gave him the singular privilege of quartering the royal arms of Spain, the castle of Castile and lion of Leon, with an archipelago and five anchors, the symbol of admiralty. At the same time the rights and privileges granted him conditionally at Granada the previous April were confirmed. He and his heirs "now and forever" were to be styled Admiral of the Ocean Sea and Viceroy and Governor of "the said islands and mainland that you have found and discovered." As Viceroy he could appoint and remove all officials in the Indies and have complete civil and criminal jurisdiction; as Admiral he would have jurisdiction over all who sailed the ocean west and south of a line from the Azores to the Cape Verdes. Admiralty jurisdiction meant that he or his deputies could handle all disputes among fishermen or merchant mariners in American waters and try all cases of mutiny, piracy, barratry, and the like. It did not imply command of a fleet, or flag rank in the navy, but nonetheless was a very high and honorable distinction.

The Admiral also worked for the Sovereigns. His famous Letter on the voyage was printed at Barcelona, in Spanish, about the time that he arrived. A Latin translation, dated 29 April, appeared shortly after in Rome. The object of this prompt publication was not so much to spread the news but to obtain papal confirmation of the lands newly discovered, as the public law of Europe then required.

Pages from the Latin edition of Columbus's famous Letter of 1493.

The Sovereigns depended on Columbus to prove that his discoveries were outside jurisdiction previously granted to the king of Portugal. Pope Alexander VI, a Spanish Borgia who owed his election to Ferdinand and Isabella, let them practically "write their own ticket" in a series of papal bulls. The third and most important, dated 4 May 1493, drew a line of demarcation along the meridian one hundred leagues (318 nautical miles) west of the Azores. All undiscovered lands east of it would belong to Portugal; all west of it, to Spain.

Columbus undoubtedly suggested this line, because he believed that compass variations changed from east to west, and that the boisterous winds of Europe gave way to the gentle trades, on or about that meridian of longitude. According to Bishop Las Casas, it was an entomological boundary as well. He observed that seamen and passengers departing from Spain were tortured by lice and fleas until they reached a hundred leagues west of the Azores, when the insects began to disappear; but upon the return passage they emerged from hiding at the same longitude "in great and disturbing numbers!" A later form of this myth described insect life as disappearing at the Equator. Readers of *Don Quixote* will remember how, in that famous voyage

in the enchanted bark, the Knight of the Rueful Countenance bids Sancho Panza search himself for vermin, in order to ascertain whether or not they have passed the Line.

Nevertheless, the line of demarcation set up by the Pope was not enforced. Portugal protested, and as the hostility of D. João II would have jeopardized their communications, Ferdinand and Isabella in the Treaty of Tordesillas (1494) consented to push the line to the meridian 370 leagues (roughly

A sketch made from the de la Cosa map (see page 60) shows the Lesser Antilles and Spanish Main, discovered by Columbus on subsequent voyages.

THE LESSER ANTILLES ON JUAN DE LA COSA'S MAP

1175 miles) west of the Cape Verde Islands. From that new division of the world, Portugal derived her title to Brazil and her claim to Newfoundland.

During the three months that Columbus resided at Barcelona, news of his discovery spread wide, by means of epistles from Italian residents of Spain, and from the printed Letter in many translations. But the news traveled very slowly beyond the Alps. The learned men of Nuremberg, center of geographical study in northern

Europe, were ignorant of it as late as July 1493, and brother Bartholomew, living near Paris, did not hear of it in time to join the Admiral's Second Voyage.

Judging from letters and chronicles, the chronicles, the items in the news that aroused the most attention were gold, the naked natives, and the opportunity to convert them. Columbus had stressed all three in his Letter, as well as opening a new trade route to China. Europe was then so short of specie that any gold strike made a uni-

A fanciful version of the "discovery" of the American mainland by Amerigo Vespucci, who was wrongly credited with this feat on an influential 1507 map drawn by the German cartographer Martin Waldseemüller (see page 107).

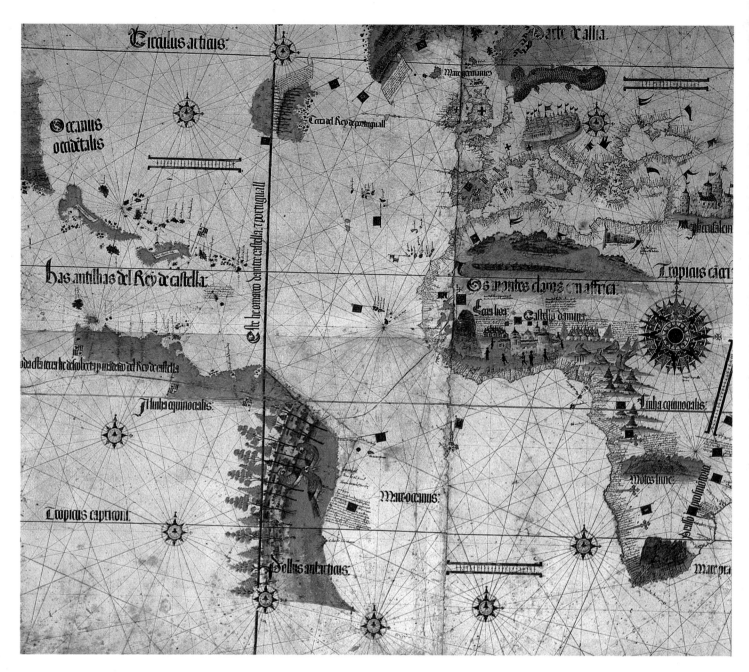

ABOVE: "The Cantino Planisphere," a map of 1502, plainly shows the line established in 1494 by the Treaty of Tordesillas.

OPPOSITE: An unlikely legend holds that this 1513 Ottoman map was partly based on a lost map drawn by Columbus himself.

versal appeal, as it would today. Fashions in 1493 required women to be heavily clothed from head to foot, so that a community where the natives wore less than a bikini for full dress was news indeed, besides suggesting the state of innocence before Adam's fall. And as Europe had an uneasy conscience at letting Christianity fall back before the Turks, this opportunity to gain souls and redress the balance aroused agreeable anticipation. Of the real significance of the discovery for Europe's future there was not one hint in contemporary comment, nor did anyone venture to suggest that Seneca's prophecy of a vast continent had been fulfilled.

Columbus's assertion that he really had reached the Indies was accepted by the Spanish Sovereigns and the Pope, but not by everyone. Peter Martyr d'Anghiera, an Italian humanist at the Spanish court, wrote to a correspondent that the size of the globe seemed to indicate that Columbus could not have reached Asia, and in November 1493 he described the Admiral in a letter to Cardinal Sforza as "Novi Orbis Repertor," "Discoverer of a New World." To him, as to other contemporaries, New World did not mean a separate, undiscovered continent, but land unknown to Ptolemy; a group of islands adjacent to the Malay Peninsula would be a New World. That is exactly the conclusion reached by Columbus himself in 1498, and by Amerigo Vespucci a little later. But Amerigo got the credit.

THE MARINER'S DAY

Time and Watches

Suppose we describe a day at sea in Columbus's time, which will also go for the entire sixteenth century. Information on this subject, since everyone then took knowledge of it for granted, is very scarce; one can only pick up bits and pieces from sea journals. Fortunately, a humorous Spanish official, Eugenio de Salazar, wrote a very detailed account of what he observed in a voyage from Spain to Santo Domingo in 1573. Without him this chapter would have been mostly blank.

A decent formality has always been observed in ships at sea. The watches are changed and the tiller or wheel is relieved according to formula, solar and stellar observations are made at fixed hours, and any departure from the settled custom is resented by mariners. In Spanish and Portuguese ships these formalities were observed with a quasi-religious ritual, which lent them a certain beauty and served to remind the seamen every half-hour of the day and night that their ship depended for safety not only on her staunchness and their own skill, but on the grace of God.

Until the late sixteenth century, the only ship's clock available was the *ampolleta* or

PAGES 100-101: It is not easy to guess what historical sources the artist drew on when he produced this strange drawing of Columbus's three ships.

RIGHT: Old-time salts would probably have disliked this Spanish compass card because it is marked off in degrees rather than directional points.

BELOW: A primitive quadrant with plumbline (r) to keep it vertical.

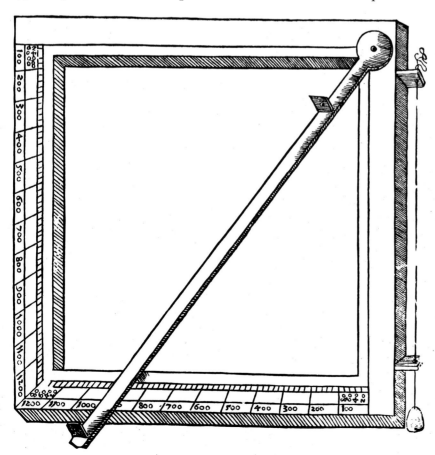

reloj de arena (sand clock), a half-hour glass containing enough sand to run from the upper to the lower section in exactly thirty minutes. Made in Venice, these glasses were so fragile that many spares were usually carried – Magellan had eighteen on his flagship. It was the duty of a ship's boy in each watch to mind the *ampolleta* and reverse it promptly when the sand ran out. A very rough sea might retard the running of the sand, or the boy might go to sleep; Columbus on one occasion expressed indignation with a lazy lad who lost count. As a ship gains time sailing east and loses it sailing west, even the most modern ship's clock has to be corrected daily by radio. The only way one could mark correct sun time in the era of discovery was to erect a pin or gnomon on the center of the compass card, and watch for the exact moment of noon when the sun's shadow touched the fleur-de-lis that marked north (or, if in the Southern Hemisphere, south) and then turn the glass. Even that could not be counted on to give true noon nearer than 15 to 20 minutes.

The *marineros, grumetes,* and *oficiales* of the ship's company (able seamen, apprentice seamen, and petty officers such as caulker and cooper) were divided into two watches (*cuartos* or *guardias*) of four hours each. An officer commanded each watch according to a fixed rule of precedence: captain, pilot, *maestre* (master), *contramaestre* (master's mate or chief boatswain).* From sundry entries in Colum-

---

*In Portuguese ships, curiously, the pilot came below master.

LEFT: Many other great sailors followed in Columbus's footsteps. Here, England's Sir Francis Drake during his 1579 discovery of California.

BELOW: This portrait of Drake now hangs in the National Portrait Gallery in London.

bus's Journal, it is clear that his watches were changed at 3, 7, and 11 o'clock. These hours seem odd to a modern seaman, who by immemorial usage expects watches to change at 4, 8, and 12 and I believe they were so changed from 1500 on. Presumably the afternoon watched was "dogged" (i.e., split into two 2-hour watches) as the merchant marine still did in the nineteenth century, in order that the men might change their hours nightly. On a sailing vessel which might be many weeks or even months at sea, it was fairer to dog the watches daily so that each man would have the unpopular "graveyard watch" from midnight to 4:00 a.m. (or from 11 to 3) on alternate nights.

Mariners in those days thought of time less in terms of hours than of *ampolletas* and *guardias*, glasses and watches, eight glasses to a watch. The system of half-hourly ships's bells that we are familiar with began as a means of accenting the turning of the glass. No ship's bell is mentioned in any of the Spanish sea journals of the sixteenth century that I have seen, and García de Palacio's *Instrucción Náutica* (1587), the Mexican seaman's first Bowditch, says nothing of them. Drake's flagship *Golden Hind* carried no bell, but his men "liberated" one from the church at Guatulco, Mexico, in 1579. They hung it in

RIGHT: A carrack of *c.* 1470 by a Flemish artist whom we know only as "W.A." It is probably very similar to *Santa Maria*.

FAR RIGHT TOP: These two small lockets are said to contain dust taken from Columbus's casket, though the authenticity of the casket itself is in some doubt.

whenever the weather was clear and the latitude not too low, your sixteenth-century navigator could tell sun time from the Guards of the North Star. The Little Bear or Little Dipper swings around Polaris once every 24 hours, side-real time. The two brightest stars of that constellation, *beta* (Kochab) and *gamma*, which mark the edge of the Dipper farthest from the North Star, were called the Guards; and if you knew where Kochab (the principal Guard) should be at midnight, you could tell time as from a clock hand. The early navigators constructed a diagram of a little man with Polaris in his belly, his forearms pointing E and W, and his shoulders NE and NW. That gave eight positions for Kochab. As this star moved from one major position to another in three hours, you could tell time at night if you

an improvised belfry on board, where a Spanish prisoner reported that it was "used to summon the men to pump." Since pumping ship was the first duty of every watch, it is evident that the bell was used for summons, and that this use of the bell was new to Spaniards, if not to Englishmen.

At night in the Northern Hemisphere

RIGHT: An evolved form of cross-staff that had some features of a quadrant, invented by English explorer John Davis around 1587.

FAR RIGHT: Navigators' instruments recovered from the wreck of the English carrack *Mary Rose*, which was sunk off Portsmouth in 1545. Any of these objects – a pair of dividers, a miniature sundial and a slate protractor – could easily have been carried on board the *Santa Maria*.

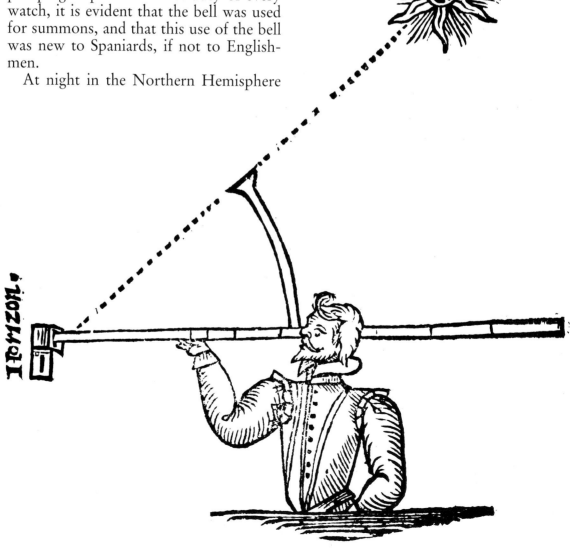

knew its position at midnight on that date. For that purpose a very simple instrument, the nocturnal, sufficed. It had a hole in the center through which you sighted Polaris, and a movable arm representing the Guards, which you moved until it pointed at Kochab; then you read the time off a scale on the outer disk. Nocturnals were in use for centuries. With a little practice, almost anyone on a long voyage can learn to tell time by this method within a quarter-hour.

Ritual and Religion

In the great days of sail, before man's inventions and gadgets had given him a false confidence in his power to conquer the ocean, seamen were the most religious of all workers on land or sea. The mariner's philosophy he took from the Vulgate's 107th Psalm: "They that go down to the sea in ships and occupy their business in great waters; these men see the works of the Lord, and his wonders in the deep. For at his word, the stormy wind ariseth, which lifteth up the waves thereof." It behooved seamen to obey the injunction of the Psalmist, "O that men would therefore praise the Lord for his goodness, and declare the wonders that he doeth for the children of men!" That is exactly what they did, after their fashion. The Protestant Reformation did not change the old custom of shipboard piety, only the ritual; Spanish prisoners on Drake's *Golden Hind* reported a daily service which featured the singing of psalms.

Although the captain or master, if no priest were present, led morning and evening prayers, the little semi-religious observances which marked almost every half-hour of the day were performed by the youngest lads on board, the *pajes de escober* (pages of the broom). This I suppose was on the same principle as having family grace said by the youngest child;

God would be better pleased by the voice of innocence.

According to Eugenio de Salazar, the ritual which he describes always prevailed when venturing on unknown seas where the divine protection was imperatively needed. No pious commander would have omitted aught of these traditional observances. I repeat them here just as Salazar reports them, with a translation.

Bendita sea la luz,
Blessed be the light of day
y la Santa Veracruz
and the Holy Cross, we say;
y el Señor de la Verdad,
and the Lord of Veritie
y la Santa Trinidad;
and the Holy Trinity
bendita sea el alma,
Blessed be th'immortal soul
y el Señor que nos la manda;
and the Lord who keeps it whole,
bendito sea el día
blessed be the light of day
y el Señor que nos lo envía.
and He who sends the night away.

He then recited *Pater Noster* and *Ave Maria*, and added:

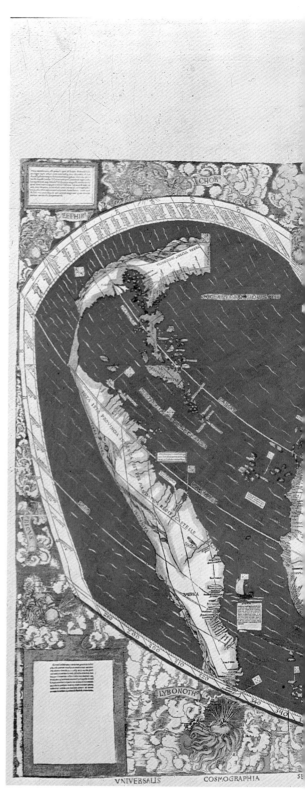

RIGHT: A page from a book by geographer Giovanni de Sacrobosco published in 1537. The ship in the background is a large carrack.

FAR RIGHT: A copy of the famous 1507 Martin Waldseemüller map that first showed the New World as a continent separate from Asia and named it "America."

Dios nos dé buenos días; buen viaje; buen pasaje haga la nao, señor Capitán y maestre y buena compaña, amén; así faza buen viaje; faza: muy buenos días dé Dios a vuestras mercedes, señores de popa y proa.

God give us good days, good voyage, good passage to the ship, sir captain and master and good company, amen; so let there be a good voyage; many good days may God grant your graces, gentlemen of the afterguard and gentlemen forward.

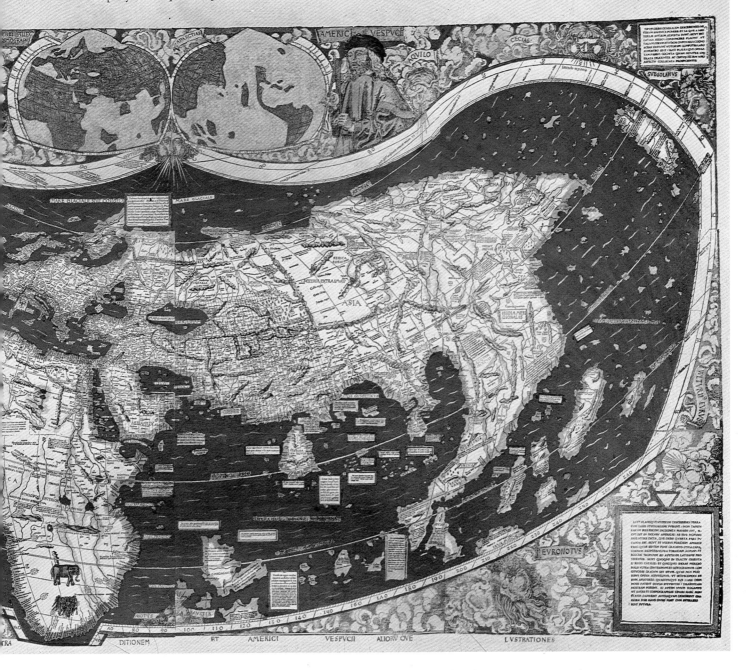

Mapa universal de 1507

(Primero con el nombre América)

Descrito por Carlos Sanz en su obra

"EL NOMBRE DE AMERICA"

Mapas y Libros que lo impusieron

Before being relieved the dawn watch was supposed to have the deck well scrubbed down with salt water hauled up in buckets, using stiff besoms made of twigs. At 6:30 or 7:30 the *ampolleta* was turned up for the seventh and last time on that watch, and the boy sang out:

Buena es la que va,
Good is that which passeth,
mejor es la que viene;
better that which cometh,
siete es pasada y en ocho muele,
seven is past and eight floweth,
mas molerá si Dios quisiere,
more shall flow if God willeth,
cuenta y pasa, que buen viaje faza.
count and pass makes voyage fast.

As soon as the sands of the eighth successive glass ran out, the boy in turning up

Twenty years after he accompanied Columbus on his Second Voyage, Juan Ponce de León, shown here sampling some water from what he hopes may be the Fountain of Youth, became famous as the discoverer of Florida.

said, instead of his usual ditty:

Al cuarto, al cuarto, señores marineros de buena parte, al cuarto, al cuarto en bueno hora de la guardia del señor piloto, que ya es hora; leva, leva.

On deck, on deck, Mr. Mariners of the right side,* on deck in good time you of Mr. Pilot's watch, for it's already time; shake a leg!

The new watch need no time to dress, for nobody has undressed; when they went below in early morn, each man sought out his favorite soft plank, or some corner wherein he could brace himself against the ship's rolling and pitching. The mariners coming on duty are soon awake, rubbing their eyes and grumbling, and each man grabs a ship biscuit, some garlic cloves, a bit of cheese, a pickled sardine, or whatever is on for breakfast, and shuffles aft to the break in the poop. The helmsman gives the course to the captain of his watch, who repeats it to the new helmsman, who repeats it again. Little chance for error! A lookout is posted forward, another aft, the off-going captain of the watch transfers his reckoning from slate to logbook, and the ship's boy wipes the slate clean for the new captain. Chips the carpenter (or *calafate* the caulker if he goes on watch) primes the pump, and if the ship has made water during the night, two or three hands pump her dry. The off-going watch eat breakfast and curl up somewhere out of the sun to sleep.

Now the decks are dry, the sun is yard-arm high, and the ship is dancing along before the trades with a bone in her teeth. The captain, whose servant has brought him a bucket of sea water, a cup of fresh water, and a bit of breakfast in his cabin, comes on deck, looks all around the horizon, ejaculates a pious *gracias a Dios* for fair weather, and chats with the master or pilot.

Each watch is responsible for the ship during its hours of duty, except in cases of tempest or accident, when all hands are summoned. The usual duties are keeping the decks both clear and clean, making and setting sail as required, trimming sheets and braces; and when there is nothing else to do, scrubbing the rails, and making spun yarn and chafing-gear out of old rope, and overhauling other gear. In the morning watch, as soon as the running rigging has dried from the night dews, it has to be swayed up, and every few days the lanyards or tackles that connect the shrouds with the bulwarks must be taken up – but not too taut.

One question to which every old salt

*Meaning the watch that is due on deck.

wants the answer is about "Crossing the Line." Since the principal southern voyages after 1498 crossed the Equator and entered the Southern Hemisphere, did they do it with ceremony? Did the Portuguese and Spanish navigators relieve the tension of a long voyage with the now time-honored ceremony of Crossing the Line? Did a burlesque Neptune and court come on board over the bows, subjecting the "pollywogs" or neophytes to various humorous indignities to turn them into "shellbacks"? Existing sources indicate that they did not; this ceremony belonged to the northern nations. It was derived from the medieval custom of Norman, Hanseatic, and Dutch sailors holding a quasi-religious service when they passed a well-known landmark such as the Pointe du Raz in Brittany or the Berlingas off Portugal.

The earliest known reference to a ceremony at the Equator is a contemporary account of the voyage of the Parmentier brothers of Dieppe to Sumatra in 1529. "Tuesday 11 May in the morning, about 50

of our people were made *chevaliers* and received the accolade in passing below the Equator; and the mass *Salve Sancta Parens* was sung from notes to mark the day's solemnity; and we took a great fish called albacore and some bonito, of which a stew was made for supper, solemnizing this feast of chivalry." The next, in order of time, occurred on the voyage of a French ship captained by Jean de Léry, to Brazil in 1557. Here is the first reference to the now traditional pranks: "This day the 4th of February, when we passed the World's Center, the sailors went through their accustomed ceremonies . . . namely, to bind [a man] with ropes and plunge him into the sea, or blacken his face well with an old rag rubbed on the bottom of the kettle and then shave it off, so as to give those who had never passed the Equator something to remember. But one can buy oneself off and be exempt from all that by paying for wine for all hands, as I did."

Parmentier's and Léry's ships were French. When did the Portuguese and Spanish adopt this genial way to break the monotony of a long voyage? Gossipy Pigafetta, who sailed with Magellan and Elcano around the world in 1519-22, never mentions anything of the sort, which suggests that they had not yet done so.

Sixty years passed, and the account by Jan Huygen van Linschoten of a voyage to Goa in an official Portuguese fleet indicates that sailors of this nation had taken over the custom and developed it in their own fashion. Linschoten's ship sailed in

ABOVE: Some sixteenth-century carpenters' tools salvaged from the *Mary Rose*. Among them: a brace, planes, a mallet, a mortice gauge and a whetstone. The particularly well-preserved iron nail in the foreground had fallen into a barrel of pitch.

LEFT: A portrait of Ponce de León taken from Herrera's 1601 *Historia General de los Hechos de los Castellanos*.

ABOVE: John Cabot, as an artist imagines him, about to set out from Bristol in the *Mathew* on the voyage in which he will discover (June 1497) the continent of North America.

OPPOSITE TOP: A 1546 map showing the areas of Canada explored by Jacques Cartier from 1534 to 1542.

OPPOSITE BOTTOM LEFT: Jacques Cartier, the great French explorer.

OPPOSITE BOTTOM RIGHT: An artist's version (complete with polar bears) of John and Sebastian Cabot first setting foot on North America.

February 1583; on 26 May she passed the Equator off Guinea, and on the 29th the business began. Each ship, following "an ancient custome," elected someone as "Emperor," who became lord of misrule. On this occasion the pranksters and the drinking went too far, and "by meanes of certain words that passed out of their mouths, there fell a great strife and contention among us at the banquet; at the least a hundred rapiers drawne, without respecting the Captaine or any other, for he lay under foote, and they trod upon him and had killed each other," had not a distinguished passenger, the new archbishop of Goa, burst forth from his cabin, and commanded every man, under pain of excommunication, to hand over his weapons. This they did, and they strife ended.

No record exists, to my knowledge, of any Spanish ship holding a Crossing the Line ceremony before the eighteenth century. The Portuguese must have adopted it from their many North European friends.

Returning to daily life at sea, on big ships the master's or pilot's orders were transmitted to the men through the *contramaestre* or chief boatswain, who carried a pipe or whistle on a lanyard around his neck and on it played a variety of signals. There is no mention of a pipe on Columbus's ships, probably because they were so small that the captain of the watch gave orders orally. Salazar said he had never seen an order so well and promptly obeyed by soldiers as those of his pilot. Let him but cry, *Ah! de proa!* (Hey, up forward!) and they all come aft on the run "like conjured demons" awaiting his pleasure. Here are some samples of the orders.

dejad las chafaldetes
well the clewlines
alzá aquel briol
heave on that buntline
empalomadle la boneta
lace on the bonnet
tomad aquel puño
lay hold of that clew
entren esas badasas aprisa por esos ollaos
pass them toggles through the latches quick
levá el papahigo
hoist the main course
izá el trinquete
raise the foresail
dad vuelta
put your back into it
enmará un poco la cebadera
give the spritsail a little sheet
desencapillá la mesana
unbend the mizzen
ligá la tricia al guindaste
belay the halyard on the bitts
tirá de los escotines de gabia
haul in on the topsail sheets
suban dos á los penoles
two of you up on the yardarm
untá los vertellos
grease the parrel trucks
amarrá aquellas burdas
belay them backstays
zafá los embornales
clear the scuppers
juegue el guimbalete para que la bomba achique
work that pump brake till she sucks

Nautical Castilian, like nautical English of the last century, had a word for everything in a ship's gear and a verb for every action; strong, expressive words that could not be misunderstood when bawled out in a gale.

A beautiful Islamic astrolabe. Meant for use by astronomers, it would probably have baffled most sailors.

o San Pedro – gran varón
o San Pablo – son compañón
o que ruegue – a Dio por nos
o por nosotros – navegantes
en este mundo – somo tantes
o ponente – digo levante
o levante – se leva el sol
o ponente – resplandor
fantineta – via lli amor
o joven home – gauditor

And so on, improvising, until the halyard is "two-blocks," when the captain of the watch commands, *Dejad la driza, amarrá* (Well the halyard, belay!).

When not ordering the men about, the captain of the watch kept the deck just forward of the binnacle. On all but the smaller vessels the helmsman had a second compass to steer by, but he could not see ahead, and so had to be an expert at the feel of the ship to keep her on her course. Salazar gives us some specimens of the orders to the helmsman:

botá a babor
port your helm
no boteis
steady
arriba
up helm
goberná la ueste cuarta al sueste
steer W by S

Besides nautical language, a nautical slang had developed. Just as modern seamen with mock contempt speak of "this wagon" or "the old crate," a Spaniard called his ship *rocín de madera* (wooden jade) or *pájaro puerco* (flying pig). The nickname for the firebox meant "pot island." People on board got in the habit of using nautical phrases for other things; Salazar, for instance, says, "When I want a pot of jam I say, *saca la cebadera*, break out the spritsail; if I want a table napkin I say, *daca el pañol*, lead me to the sail-locker. If you wish to eat or drink in form I say, *pon la mesana*, set the mizzen. When a mariner upsets a jug he says, *oh! cómo achicais*, Oh how she sucks! When one breaks wind, as often happens, someone is sure to cry, *Ah! de popa*, Hey there, aft!"

For any lengthy operation like winding in the anchor cable or hoisting a yard, the seamen had an appropriate *saloma* or chantey, and of these Salazar gives an example which it is useless to translate. The chanteyman sang or shouted the first half of each line, the men hauled away on the "o" and joined in on the second half, while they got a new hold on the halyard:

Bu izá
o dio – ayuta noy
o que somo – servi soy
o voleamo – ben servir
o la fede – mantenir
o la fede – de cristiano
o malmeta – lo pagano
sconfondi – y sarrahin
torchi y mori – gran mastín
o fillioli – dabrahin
o non credono – que ben sia
o non credono – la fe santa
en la santa – fe di Roma
o di Roma – está el perdón

Naturally there was a good deal of joking about the seats hung over the rail forward and aft, for the seamen and afterguard to ease themselves. These were called *jardines*, perhaps in the memory of the usual location of the family privy. Salazar writes in mock sentiment of the lovely views they afforded of moon and planets, and of the impromptu washings that he there obtained from the waves. A later voyager, Antonio de Guevara, complained of the indecency of thus exposing a Very Reverend Lord Bishop to the full view of the ship's company, and adverts bitterly to the tarred rope-end which performed the function assigned by North American folklore to the corncob.

Food and Drink

Apparently the seamen on Spanish and Portuguese ships enjoyed but one hot meal a day. This must have come around noon, so that the watch below could get theirs before coming on deck, and the watch relieved could eat after them.

Who did the cooking? I wish I knew! There was no rating of cook on any of Columbus's ships or even on Magellan's. The earliest man especially designated as

This sixteenth-century print purports to show a scene from the Third Voyage in which Indian divers gather pearls for Columbus's fleet. In fact, although he knew that the waters between Venezuela and Margarita I. were rich in pearls, Columbus never paused to try to harvest them.

RIGHT: Some domestic items used by sailors on board the *Mary Rose*. The wreck of this ship is yielding invaluable information about life at sea in the early sixteenth century.

BELOW: A time-telling nocturnal. Polaris is sighted through the center-hole, and the arm is moved to point to Kochab. The time can then be read off the pre-set scale on the outer disc.

cook that I have found on a ship's roll sailed on Sebastian Cabot's flagship in 1526. García de Palacio's *Instrucción Náutiva* of 1587, which gives all ratings and tells everyone's duties mentions neither cook nor cooker; although the steward, he says, has charge of the fire. My guess is that the hard-worked ship's boys took turns at the firebox, except that the captain's servant would naturally have cooked for him, and pages of gentlemen volunteers served them. On board the big Mexico-bound galleons described by Palacio, a table was set for the men forward, the boatswain presided, and the pages served and cleared away. On small ships it is probable that foremast hands took their share in a wooden bowl and ate it with their fingers wherever they could find a place. How the little *fogón* or open firebox could cook food for over a hundred people on a small caravel, as it must have on *Niña*'s voyage home in 1496, staggers the imagination.

The only drinks mentioned in Spanish or Portuguese inventories are water and wine, both of which were kept in various types of wooden casks. It was the cooper's job to see that these were kept tight and well stowed or lashed down so that they would not roll. South Europeans, unlike the English and French, did not carry beer or cider, which always went sour on a long

fared as well as peasants or workers ashore, except during a storm, or weather so rough that no fire could be kept – or when provisions brought from Europe gave out.

Dinner for the afterguard was announced by a ship's boy in this wise:

Tabla, tabla, señor capitán y maestra y buena compaña, tabla puesta; vianda presta; agua usada para el señor capitán y maestre y buena compaña. Viva, Viva el Rey de Castilla por mar y por tierra! Quien le diere guerra que le corten la cabeza; quien no dijere amén, que no le den á beber. Tabla en buena hora, quien no viniere que no coma.

Table, table, sir captain and master and good company, table ready; meat ready;

LEFT: Even as simple an instrument as the humble sundial could be a useful aid to navigation.

BELOW: Two eighteenth-century descendants of the quadrant were the quintant and octant, developed by England's John Hadley.

voyage; coffee and tea did not reach Europe until the following century. The staff of life for Spanish seamen was wine, olive oil, salt meat, salt codfish, and bread in the form of sea biscuit or hardtack baked ashore from wheat flour and stowed in the driest part of the ship. The only sweetening came in the form of honey, sugar being too expensive. Columbus's ideas of the proper provisioning of vessels on an American voyage are given in a letter to the Sovereigns of about 1498-1500:

Victualling them should be done in this manner: the third part of the breadstuff to be good biscuit, well seasoned and not old, or the major portion will be wasted; a third part of salted flour, salted at the time of milling; and a third part of wheat. Further there will be wanted wine, salt meat, oil, vinegar, cheese, chickpeas, lentils, beans, salt fish and fishing tackle, honey, rice, almonds, and raisins.

Olive oil, carried in huge earthenware jars, was used for cooking fish, meat, and legumes. Salted flour could be made into unleavened bread and cooked in the ashes, as Arab seamen do today. Barreled salt sardines and anchovies are frequently mentioned among ships' stores of the time, and garlic would certainly not have been forgotten. The sixteenth-century mariners

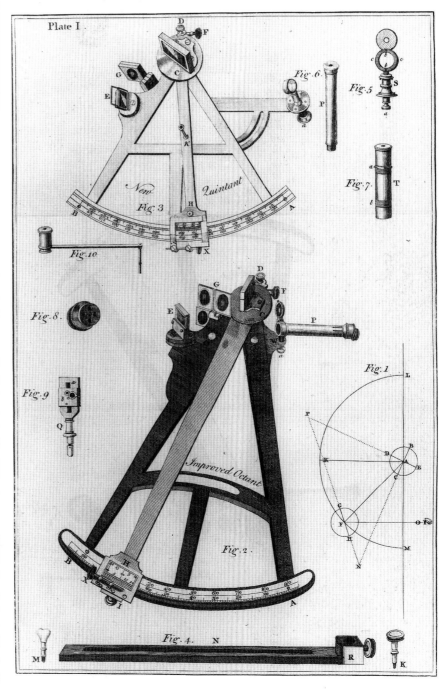

water as usual for sir captain and master and good company. Long live the King of Castile by land and sea! Who says to him war, off with his head; who won't say amen, gets nothing to drink. Table is set, who don't come won't eat.

Salazar describes how the pages would slam on the officers' table a great wooden dish of string, ill-cooked salt meat, when everyone would grab his share and attack it with a sheath knife as if he were a practioner of anatomy; and how every bone was left "clean as ivory." The table conversation, he says, was mostly sighing for what you couldn't have – "Oh! how I'd fancy a bunch of Guadalajara white grapes! – I could manage a few turnips of Somo Sierra! – If we only had on board a plate of Ilescas strawberries!"

What they longed for, obviously, were anti-scorbutics. Nothing then was known about vitamins, and, for the of fresh vegetables, fruit, or fruit juice, scurvy in its most hideous forms raged among the seamen on almost every long voyage. The officers fared better, as they always carried personal luxuries such as figs, raisins, prunes, and pots of jam which kept the dread disease away. By the end of the next century (as Abbé Labat tells us) the French managed to sail with salad plants set out in flats, so that the afterguard enjoyed green salad almost daily; but they had to set a twenty-four hour guard over their shipboard garden to keep off rats and sailors.

Although Chaunu's compilation of voyages to the Indies mentions several instances of food giving out on an unduly long return voyage, that was comparatively rare on the West Indies routes. But no master mariner prior to Drake managed to

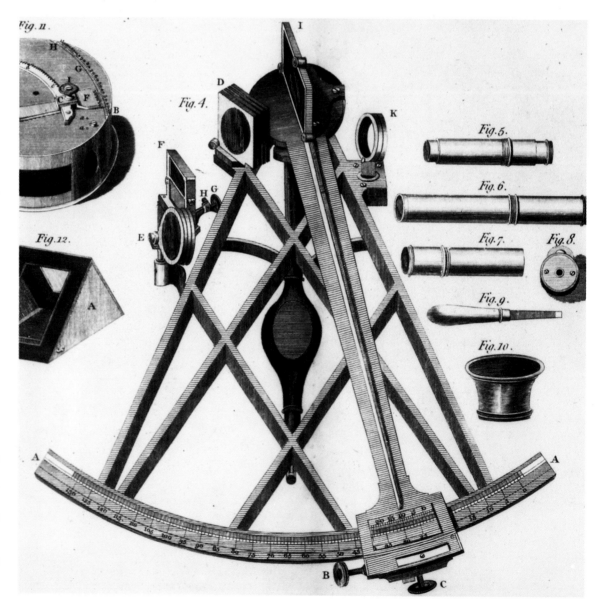

The sextant was the last step in the long evolution of the old quadrant. Invented by John Hadley in the mid-eighteenth century, it could measure angles up to 130° with great precision. It was so named because its arch or curved "limb" was one sixth of a circle.

The costume that this artist has given his smug-looking Columbus would be appropriate if he had lived at the time of the Spanish Armada instead of 100 years earlier.

feed his crew adequately on voyages that went south of the Line, especially those which reached the Pacific. There simply was not room enough, or storage tight enough, to preserve basic foodstuffs such as wine, hard bread, flour, and salt meat for so long a time. Hence the resort to penguin meat, seal, and other loathsome substitutes; and occasionally to the desperate eating of rats and chewing leather chafing-gear. Drake's men made out comparatively well, only because he stripped every prize ship of all desirable food stores, gear, and weapons. There is not one of these southern voyages on which the modern blue-water yachtsman, used to refrigeration and canned goods, would have been happy.

Navigation

During the sixteenth century, "rutters," manuals of navigation, such as Medina's *Arte de Navegar* (1545), proliferated; but sailors, the most conservative of men, were

When she sank in 1545 *Mary Rose* was some 35 years old. Thus many of her fittings may be very similar to those on Columbus's vessels. Among these rigging items salvaged from *Mary Rose* are bronze sheaves, blocks (the long one being a shoe block, with sheaves at right angles), trucks and a spacer (center left) from a parrel that supported a yard and a deadeye (lower right) that secured the lower end of a shroud.

reluctant to try anything new. It was the pilot's business to keep track of the ship's position; but despite the education given pilots before they could be licensed as such, throughout the sixteenth century most pilots depended on dead reckoning.

Captain Teixeira da Mota, after meticulous search into both manuscript and printed rutters of the sixteenth century, has concluded convincingly that the best Portuguese pilots early in the century had plotted the trade winds (which they called *os ventos gerais*), as well as the equatorial current which runs from the bulge of Africa to the Caribbean. They pointed out very early the important fact – known to any square-rig master in the last century – that vessels sailing from the Cape Verde Islands to Brazil must not allow themselves to be carried to the north (leeward) to Cape San Roque, but steer for Cabo Santo Agostinho. Similarly, the Spaniards, owing to their increasing trade with Hispaniola, Cuba, and Mexico, found out about the Gulf Stream and so planned their return routes to Spain that this mighty ocean current would help them to whip around Florida and up into the zone of the westerlies.

If one studies the rutters rather than actual voyages, one too easily concludes

that Portuguese pilots of the sixteenth century knew everything. But when we read the *Tratado da Sphera* of 1537 by Pedro Nunes (Nonius), the famous Portuguese-Jewish mathematician who discovered the vernier, we wonder how useful these pilots really were. "Why do we put up with these pilots, with their bad language and barbarous manners?" wrote Nunes. "They know neither sun, moon nor stars, nor their courses, movements or declinations; neither latitude not longitude of the places on the globe, nor astrolabes, quadrants, cross staffs or watches, nor years common or bissextile, equinoxes or solstices." Yet they were supposed to have learned all these things before being licensed by the Casa de Contratación, or by the corresponding board at Lisbon.

Columbus was a dead-reckoning navigator. He made colossal mistakes every time he tried to determine latitude from a star until, marooned at Jamaica, he had plenty of time to make repeated observations. He knew no way (nor did anyone else in the sixteenth century) of determining longitude except by timing an eclipse. Regiomontanus's *Ephemerides* and Zacuto's *Almanach Perpetuum* gave the predicted hours of total eclipses at Nuremberg and

Salamanca respectively, and by comparing those with the observed hour of the eclipse by local sun time, multiplying by 15 to convert time into arc, you could find the longitude west of the almanac-maker's meridian. This sounds simple enough, but Columbus with two opportunities (1494 and 1503) muffed both, as did almost everyone else for a century. At Mexico City in 1541 a mighty effort was made by the intelligentsia to determine the longitude of that place by timing two eclipses of the moon. The imposing result was 8h 2m 32s (120° 38′) west of Toledo; but the correct difference of longitude between the two places is 95° 12′. Thus the Mexican savants made an error of some 25½ degrees, putting their city into the Pacific! Even in the late seventeenth century Père Labat, the earliest writer (to my knowledge) to give the position of Hispaniola correctly, adds this caveat: "I only report the longitude to warn the reader that nothing is more uncertain, and that no method used up to the present to find longitude has produced anything fixed and certain."

Dead-reckoning is still the foundation of celestial navigation, but the modern navigator checks his D.R. daily (if weather permits) by latitude or longitude sights or both, which Columbus never learned to do. And, as an error of half a point in your course will mean an error of about 250 miles in landfall on an ocean crossing, it is evident that Columbus's dead-reckoning was extraordinarily careful and accurate. Andrés Bernáldez, who had information directly from the Admiral after his Second Voyage, wrote, "No one considers himself a good pilot and master who, although he has to pass from one land to another very distant without sighting any other land, makes an error of 10 leagues, even in a crossing of 1000 leagues, unless the force of the tempest drives and deprives him of the use of his skill." No such dead-reckoning navigators exist today; no man alive, limited to the instruments and means at Columbus's disposal, could obtain anything near the accuracy of his results.

By the time Magellan sailed, in 1519, great advances had been made in taking meridian altitudes of the sun with a quadrant or mariner's astrolabe, and working out latitude from a simple formula. Albo, Magellan's pilot whose logbook we have,

recorded latitudes of newly discovered places fairly accurately. And there was considerable improvement during the century, as we can ascertain by the positions recorded in Drake's voyage.

The most surprising thing about Columbus's voyages, after his uncanny perception of profitable courses, was the speed that his vessels made; *Niña* and *Pinta*, for instance, making 600 miles in four days of February 1493 and approaching a speed of 11 knots. He and the Pinzón brothers must have been what men in the clipper ship era called "drivers," not comfortable joggers-along; they refused to shorten sail every night or at the appearance of every black cloud. On his first two voyages Columbus made the Grand Canary in six and seven days from Andalusia; compare that with the average time of that run for Spanish merchantmen in the half-century 1550–1600 – just double. His first ocean crossings of 2500 to 2700 nautical miles – 33 days in 1492, 29 days in 1493, 40 days on the Third Voyage in 1498, were good; and that of 21 days on the Fourth Voyage, 1502, was phenomenal. According to Pierre Chaunu, it has seldom been equaled and never surpassed in the colonial era. Even the twelve-ship convoy under Antonio de Torres, by following his master's directions, arrived

Columbus's landing on Watling Island as seen from the Indian point of view.

home in 35 days from Isabela, a record never equaled under sail. For 53 homeward-bound convoys from Havana, 1551-1650, the average time was over 67 days.

Part of the explanation of these remarkable bursts and sensational stretches of speed lies in the lines and sail plan of the caravel. Would that one of these brave little vessels were dug up, like the Viking ships in Norway, so we could guess at her secret! Naturally a lightly laden caravel, in the early voyages, could sail around a heavily laden 200- or 300-tun *nao* on the later trade routes. But the design of those full-rigged and wide-hulled ships also improved through the century. The "round tuck" at the stern of the first *Santa Maria* gave way to a square stern, upon which the high superstructure was built, as an integral part of the vessel. Toward the end of the century, the Dutch began to save man-power by cutting sails smaller and shortening the yards. Perhaps the most important improvement was that of sheathing, to thwart the teredos. Drake's flagship was double-planked, and toward the end of the century Henri IV of France, when outfitting a fleet against Spain, insisted on not only double sheathing but a pad of superior German felt between the planks, and copper-plating below the waterline.

End of a Day at Sea

At 3:00 or 4:00 p.m. the first dog watch is set. The day's work of scrubbing, splicing, seizing, and making repairs is now done; and if the wind is such that the sails need no handling before nightfall, the men sit about talking and spinning yarns, tending a fish-line, washing in buckets of salt water. Peninsula seamen were a cleanly lot.

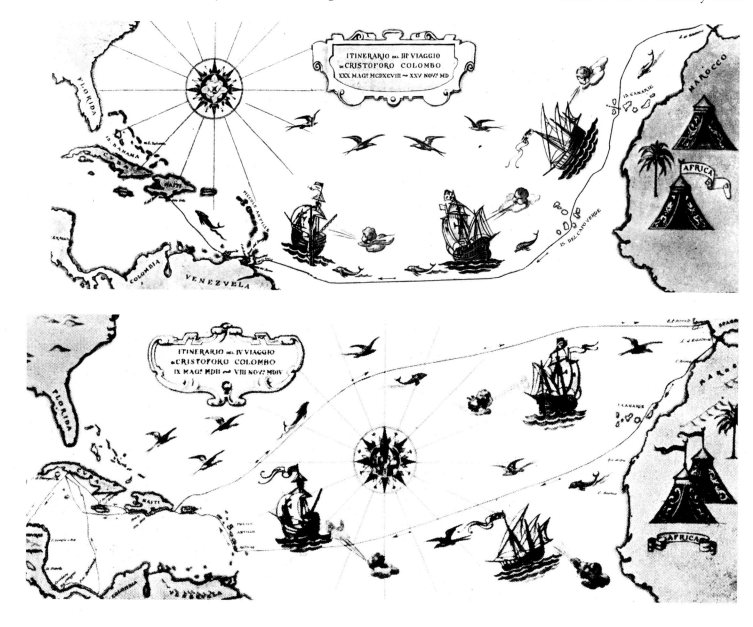

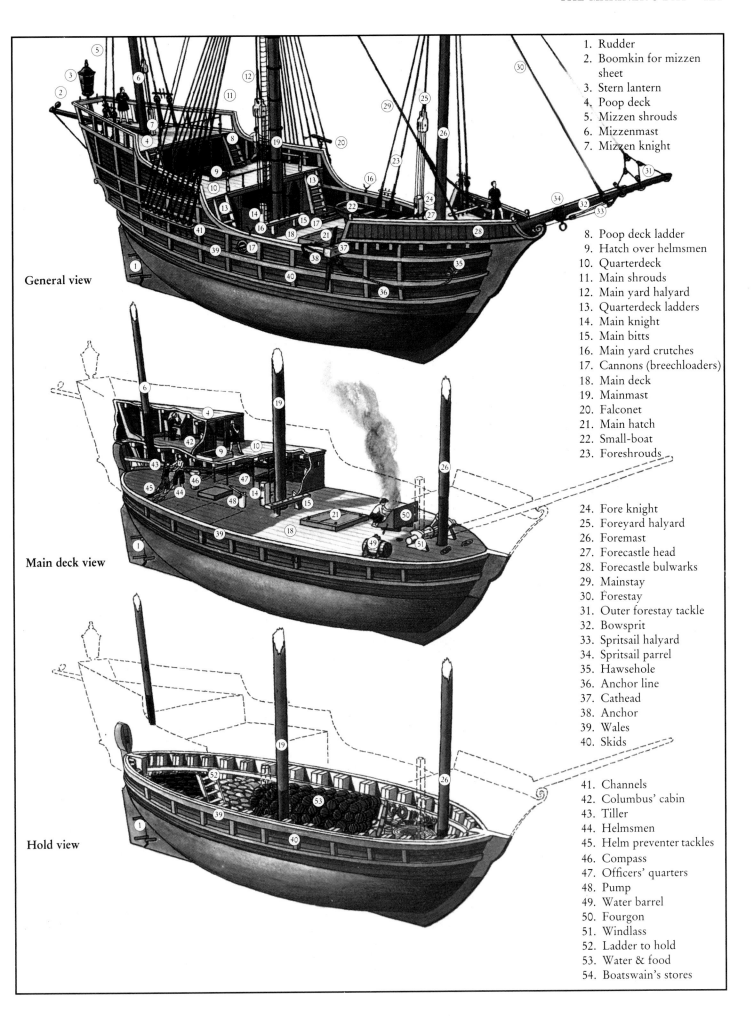

General view

Main deck view

Hold view

1. Rudder
2. Boomkin for mizzen sheet
3. Stern lantern
4. Poop deck
5. Mizzen shrouds
6. Mizzenmast
7. Mizzen knight

8. Poop deck ladder
9. Hatch over helmsmen
10. Quarterdeck
11. Main shrouds
12. Main yard halyard
13. Quarterdeck ladders
14. Main knight
15. Main bitts
16. Main yard crutches
17. Cannons (breechloaders)
18. Main deck
19. Mainmast
20. Falconet
21. Main hatch
22. Small-boat
23. Foreshrouds

24. Fore knight
25. Foreyard halyard
26. Foremast
27. Forecastle head
28. Forecastle bulwarks
29. Mainstay
30. Forestay
31. Outer forestay tackle
32. Bowsprit
33. Spritsail halyard
34. Spritsail parrel
35. Hawsehole
36. Anchor line
37. Cathead
38. Anchor
39. Wales
40. Skids

41. Channels
42. Columbus' cabin
43. Tiller
44. Helmsmen
45. Helm preventer tackles
46. Compass
47. Officers' quarters
48. Pump
49. Water barrel
50. Fourgon
51. Windlass
52. Ladder to hold
53. Water & food
54. Boatswain's stores

Columbus, at least twice on his First Voyage, mentions their going swimming in a mid-ocean calm, and they never missed a chance to wash themselves and their clothes upon landing near a river. They certainly needed it, since hygiene (in the sixteenth century) required them to wear woolen clothes from neck to feet no matter how hot the climate.

In the second dog watch and before the first night watch is set, all hands are called to evening prayers. The ceremony begins with a ship's boy trimming the binnacle lamp and singing, as he brings it aft along the deck:

> *Amén, Dios nos dé buenas noches, buen viaje, buen pasaje haga la nao, Señor Capitán y Maestre y buena compaña.*
>
> Amen. God give us a good night and good sailing; may the ship make a good passage, Sir Captain and Master and good company.

The boys then lead the ship's company in what was technically called *la doctrina cristiana.* All hands say *Pater Noster, Ave Maria,* and *Credo,* and sing *Salve Regina.* This beautiful hymn, one of the oldest Benedictine chants, fittingly closed the day. The music has come down to us so that we can in some measure re-create that ancient hymn of praise to the Queen of Heaven that floated over uncharted waters every evening as a fleet of discovery slipped along.

We are not to suppose that the seamen kept very close to this music. Columbus once refers to the "*Salve Regina,* which the seamen sing, or say after their own fashion," and Salazar wrote his friend: "Presently begins the *Salve,* and we are all singers, for we all have a throat. . . For as mariners are great friends of divisions, and divide the four winds into thirty-two, so the eight tones of music they distribute into thirty-two other and different tones, perverse, resonant, and very dissonant, as if we had today in the singing of the *Salve* and *Litany* a tempest of hurricanes of music, so that if God and His glorious Mother and the Saints to whom we pray should look down upon our tones and voices and not on our hearts and spirits, it would not do to beseech mercy with such a confusion of bawlings!"

The boatswain or boatswain's mate, whichever is on watch, extinguishes the cooking fire before the first night watch is set. As the *ampolleta* is turned up, the boy chorister sings:

> *Bendita la hora en que Dios nació*
> Blessed be the hour in which God was born
> *Santa María que le parió*
> Saint Mary who bore Him
> *San Juan que le bautizó*
> Saint John who baptized Him.
> *La guarda es tomada,*
> The watch is called,
> *La ampolleta muele,*
> The glass floweth;
> *buen viaje haremos*
> We shall make a good voyage
> *si Dios quisiere.*
> if God willeth.

On sail the ships through the soft tropic night. Every half hour the boy turns his *ampolleta* and sings his little ditty:

> *Una va pasada*
> One glass is gone
> *y en dos muele*
> and now the second floweth
> *más molerá*
> more shall run down
> *si mi Dios querrá*
> if my God willeth.
> *á mi Dios pidamos,*
> To my God let's pray
> *que bien viaje hagamos;*
> to give us good voyage;
> *y á la que es Madre de Dios y abogada nuestra,*
> and through His blessed Mother our advocate on high,
> *que nos libre de agua de bomba y tormenta*
> protect us from the waterspout and send no tempest nigh.

Then he calls to the lookout forward:
Ah! de proa, alerta, buena guardia! Hey you! forward, look alive, keep good watch.

At which the lookout was supposed to make a shout or grunt to prove that he was awake (like our "Lights burning brightly, sir!"). Every hour the helm and the lookout are relieved, but the captain of the watch keeps the quarterdeck for the whole watch, pacing up and down and peering into the binnacle to see if the helmsman is holding his course. If the night is quiet, all members of the watch not on lookout or at the helm lean over the fore bulwarks, watching entranced the phosphorescent sea, dreaming of epic morrows in that marvelous New and Other World.

OPPOSITE: A plaster relief of Christopher Columbus prepared for Chicago's Columbia Exhibition of 1893.

EDITOR'S AFTERWORD

CHRISTOPHORO COLOMBO

The features that have conventionally been assigned to Columbus are well captured in this lithograph from an old Italian book.

So spectacular was Columbus's epic First Voyage to the New World that we may sometimes forget that he led three more expeditions across the Atlantic, each adding impressively to the total of his discoveries, though not, alas, to his reputation in the Spanish court. The second trip was being planned – now with the Crown's enthusiastic support – within a month of Columbus's triumphal return in 1493. This time the Admiral had no lack of volunteers to accompany him, and when, in September, he set sail on his Second Voyage, it was at the head of a small armada of 17 ships.

The crossing was remarkably swift and uneventful, and the fleet made its first New World landfall at Dominica (Columbus's name for the island) on 3 November. Often pausing to explore, the fleet slowly made its way up the Leeward Island chain to Puerto Rico and then across the Mona Passage to Hispaniola (Santo Domingo). There Columbus found that his trading outpost on the north coast, Navidad, had been destroyed by Indians. After setting up a new post, named Isabela, farther east, he sent 12 of his ships back to Spain, thus augmenting the supplies available to the remaining five. Between April and September 1494 he explored the southern coast of Cuba, dis-

The illustrator of the 1493 edition of the Columbus Letter to Sanchez visualizes Indians fleeing at the sight of Spanish ships.

covered Jamaica, and completed his survey of the coasts of Hispaniola. After being reinforced by other ships sent from Spain, he spent the next year subduing Indian resistance on Hispaniola and establishing complete Spanish control over the island. Finally, naming his brother Bartholomew governor in his absence, Columbus sailed home in the Niña in March 1496.

Although disappointed by Columbus's failure either to locate significant sources of gold or to establish contact with the court of Cathay, the Spanish Sovereigns authorized the Admiral to make still another voyage, and in May 1498 he set forth again, this time at the head of a six-ship flotilla (three earmarked for exploration and three for the replenishment of Hispaniola). He made his landfall on 31 July at Trinidad (also named by Columbus) and subsequently sailed along the coast of present-day Venezuela. This was his first contact with the American mainland. When, after some days, he realized that this must be a continent rather than another island, he described it in his journal as an "Other World" (otro mundo) and speculated that it might be the fabled Garden of Eden.

When Columbus finally arrived at Hispaniola on 31 August he found the colony racked by civil war. He was still trying to restore order when a royal commissioner arrived from Spain. The commissioner, after hearing the complaints of the mutineers, ordered Columbus and his two brothers back to Spain to stand trial. Although all three were ultimately acquitted and restored to most of their former honors, they were never again allowed to exercise important political authority in the Indies.

Ferdinand and Isabella did, however, authorize the 50-year-old Columbus to make one more exploratory expedition, and in May 1502 he set out once again with a four-ship squadron on his Fourth (and last) Voyage. His transatlantic passage of 21 days set a record that stood for many years. He made his landfall in the Windwards, at Martinique, and then sailed up the Lesser Antilles chain until he reached Hispaniola. There he requested permission of the new governor, Ovando, to anchor in the harbor off the colonial capital of Santo Domingo, saying that he feared a hurricane was impending. But Ovando, no friend of Columbus, contemptuously refused permission and derided the Admiral's weather warning as "soothsaying." Columbus hurriedly moved his ships west along the coast until he found a suitable anchorage in a deserted estuary and waited. The hurricane materialized as predicted. Nineteen of Ovando's ships were lost with all hands, and 10 more sank with some survivors; Columbus's four ships were unscathed.

Columbus then sailed his little squadron along the southern shores of Jamaica and Cuba and thence southwest to the coast of Honduras, which he reached on 31 July 1502. For the remainder of the year he explored the coast of Central America south to the Isthmus of Panama and the present-day Colombian border. He could not know that along a considerable stretch of this route he was within only a few miles of discovering the Pacific Ocean.

He spent most of the following spring vainly trying to establish a permanent trading post on this forbidding coast, but geography, bad weather and Indian hostility frustrated all his efforts. Finally, in May 1503, the discouraged and ailing Admiral sailed the squadron – now down to two barely seaworthy ships – back into the Caribbean, bound for Hispaniola.

He got only as far as Jamaica. There both of his worn-out ships foundered, and Columbus and his men were stranded on the island for over a year. When they were finally rescued in June 1504 disease and violent factional fighting among the crew had reduced their number by about 10 percent. Once back in Santo Domingo, Columbus was able to charter a ship, and this eventually returned him to Spain in early November. In all, his final voyage to the new World had consumed two and a half years.

The Fourth Voyage may have added importantly to man's geographic knowledge and have been an epic of seamanship, but at home it was again perceived as a failure. Columbus was now largely – if still

benignly – ignored by the court, the more so as King Ferdinand became irritated by his increasingly shrill claims to a greater share of the considerable wealth beginning to flow back from the Indies. Perhaps, had he lived long enough, his fortunes might have risen again, but he was running short of time. His health, never fully restored after the trials of the Fourth Voyage, began seriously to fail, and on 20 May 1506, only 18 months after his return to Spain, he died in Valladolid. The court did not bother to send a representative to his funeral, nor did the official chronicle see fit to make a note of his passing.

How Columbus's reputation was restored and what we think of his accomplishments today have not been better summarized than by Admiral Morison:

A nineteenth-century artist imagines the scene when, at the end of the Third Voyage, Columbus is returned to Spain in chains on board *La Gorda*.

Another nineteenth-century contribution to the iconography of the Columbus legend: the lonely death of the great discoverer.

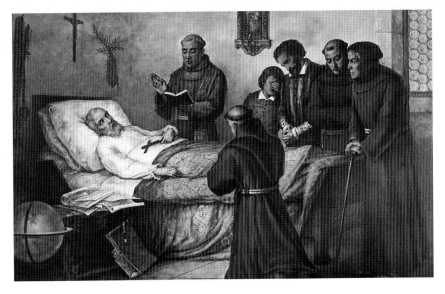

Little by little, as his life receded into history and the claims of others to be the "real" discovers of America faded into the background, his great achievements began to be appreciated. Yet it is one of the ironies of history that the Admiral himself died ignorant of what he had really accomplished, still insisting he had discovered a large number of islands, a province of China, and an "Other World"; but of the vast extent of that Other World, and of the ocean that lay between it and Asia, he had neither knowledge nor suspicion.

Now, more than five hundred years after his birth, when the day of Columbus's first landfall in the New World is celebrated throughout the length and breadth of the Americas, his fame and reputation may be considered secure, despite the efforts of armchair navigators and nationalist maniacs to denigrate him. A glance at a map of the Caribbean may remind you of what he accomplished: discovery of the Bahamas, Cuba, and Hispaniola on the First Voyage; discovery of the Lesser Antilles, Puerto Rico, Jamaica, and the south coast of Cuba on his Second, as well as founding a permanent European colony; discovery of Trinidad and the Spanish Main, on his Third; and on the Fourth Voyage, Honduras, Nicaragua, Costa Rica, Panama, and Colombia. No navigator in history, not even Magellan, discovered so much territory hitherto unknown to Europeans. None other so

effectively translated his north-south experience under the Portuguese flag to the first east-west voyage, across the Atlantic. None other started so many things from which stem the history of the United States, of Canada, and of a score of American republics.

And do not forget that sailing west to the Orient was his idea, pursued relentlessly for six years before he had the means to try it. As a popular jingle on the occasion of the four hundreth anniversary put it:

> What if wise men as far back as Ptolemy
> Judged that the earth like an orange was round,
> None of them ever said, "Come along, follow me,
> Sail to the West and the East will be found."

Columbus had his faults, but they were largely the defects of qualities that made him great. These were an unbreakable faith in God and his own destiny as the bearer of the Word to lands beyond the seas; an indomitable will and stubborn persistence despite neglect, poverty, and ridicule. But there was no flaw, no dark side to the most outstanding and essential of all his qualities – seamanship. As a master mariner and navigator, no one in the generation prior to Magellan could touch Columbus. Never was a title more justly bestowed than the one which he most jealously guarded – *Almirante del Mar Océano* – Admiral of the Ocean Sea.

BELOW RIGHT: One of many mysteries that surround Columbus is the whereabouts of his remains. This tomb in the Seville Cathedral is his official grave, but it is probably not the real one.

BELOW: Of the several places where Columbus might be buried, the most likely is here, in the Cathedral in Santo Domingo.

INDEX